THE MASHPEE INDIANS

THE Iroquois AND THEIR NEIGHBORS

LAURENCE M. HAUPTMAN
Series Editor

THE MASHPEE INDIANS

Tribe on Trial

JACK CAMPISI

SYRACUSE UNIVERSITY PRESS

Copyright © 1991 by Syracuse University Press
Syracuse, New York, 13244-5160

All Rights Reserved

First Edition 1991
91 92 93 94 95 96 97 98 99   6 5 4 3 2 1

Library of Congress Cataloging-in-Publication Data

Campisi, Jack.
    The Mashpee Indians : tribe on trial / Jack Campisi.
        p.   cm. — (The Iroquois and their neighbors)
    Includes bibliographical references and index.
    ISBN 0-8156-2517-0
    1. Mashpee Indians—Legal status, laws, etc. 2. Mashpee Indians—
Government relations. 3. Mashpee Indians—History.
4. Ethnohistory—Massachusetts. I. Title. II. Series.
E99.M4C36   1991
974.4'92—dc20   90-26976
                                                        CIP

Manufactured in the United States of America

To my wife, Beverly

Jack Campisi is Associate Professor of Anthropology at Wellesley College. He is the coeditor of *Extending the Rafters: Interdisciplinary Approaches to Iroquoian Studies* and *The Oneida Indian Experience* (Syracuse University Press).

CONTENTS

ILLUSTRATIONS
following page 78

PREFACE

It has been twelve years since the decision in *Mashpee Tribe v. New Seabury, et al.*, time enough to reflect on the meaning and significance of the events surrounding this case in which I participated. The suit concerned the issue of whether the Mashpee Wampanoag Indians of Cape Cod constituted a tribe for the purposes of the Indian Trade and Intercourse Acts. A jury found that they did not. Based on the jury's deliberations, U.S. District Court Judge Walter Skinner ruled that the Mashpees lacked standing to sue for land taken from them in contravention of federal law. He found that although the Mashpees may be a tribe for some purposes, they were not a tribe where land and federal law were concerned.

In the years since the decision, a number of Indian groups have achieved federal recognition of their tribal status either by congressional action or the more laborious and byzantine route of petitioning the Department of the Interior. A few have settled their land claims with the municipalities and private property owners they had sued, either by special legislation after the bureau's determination of the existence of a relationship with the United States or as part of their recognition by Congress.

The Mashpees, however, remain in limbo. Unwilling to accept the verdict of the district court and faced with an implacable foe — the town — they have sought justice through continued litigation, bringing to bear a variety of legal arguments, all to no avail.

While the litigation continued, I did not feel it appropriate to raise the issues addressed in this book. The legal efforts have now ceased, however, or, more properly, have been dismissed by Judge Skinner, and the Mashpees are now seeking federal acknowledgment through the administrative process. Thus it is time to discuss that case and at least a few of the issues that have troubled me and others who participated in the trial.

In writing this book I have intentionally limited my discussion of the trial to the questions and arguments of the attorneys, the testimony of the expert witnesses, and the opinions expressed by the judge. I have not included the many references to the Mashpee people, whose testimony enriched the record and whose demeanor under cross-examination was far more exemplary and dignified than that of their interrogators. This omission is not based on any assessment that one type of testimony was more valuable than another. Instead, my primary interest lies in the manner in which the anthropological theories of tribe articulated with legal equivalents and the way in which anthropological and historical data were used and abused in a courtroom setting. Of equal importance, I wish to present a summary of the tribe's history so that others might judge the merits of its claim.

Over the intervening years the Mashpee case has developed a literature of its own. Even before the completion of the appeals process, Paul Brodeur (1978) published an article in the *New Yorker* magazine. Brodeur had visited the Mashpee community in the 1960s and had written an article for the magazine, which had not been published. The trial offered an excellent opportunity to update that article. Brodeur later combined the article with one about the Passamaquoddies and published both in 1985 under the title *Restitution*. His style is reportage, anecdotal, and clearly sympathetic to the tribe. His work was followed by a book written by Francis G. Hutchins, entitled *Mashpee: the Story of Cape Cod's Indian Town*. In this work, Hutchins laid out the facts of the case from the perspective of the defendants (Hutchins was their principal scholarly witness), while arguing that "a strong and stable Indian presence in Mashpee's future seems attainable because of the unyielding commitment of so many to this goal" (Hutchins 1979: 193). To some, this conclusion seemed a tacit recognition of the existence of a tribe. Most recently, James Clifford, in a critique of anthropological theory, included a chapter on the Mashpee case based on his impressions at the time of the trial. Clifford made no attempt to research the record, review the documents, or interview the participants. Rather than detailing the events of the dispute and the evidence, Clifford was concerned with the process by which information is interpreted, how an event is perceived by the different parties to a dispute. Through it all, Clifford came away convinced "the Indians living in Mashpee and those who return regularly should be recognized as a 'tribe'" (Clifford 1988:336).

If the Mashpees are Indians (and I believe they are), and if they constitute a tribe (and I believe they do), then why did we fail so dismally in convincing a jury? Does the fault lie with the experts, the legal advocates, or the judicial system? Was this a case beyond the ability of the system to suppress its biases? Was it too threatening, to unsettling for the jury and judge? Were anthropological and historical facts irrelevant in the face of such an extraordinary remedy as the return of private title to an Indian tribe? Although I have attempted to answer these questions, I fear some remain elusive.

In completing this study I wish to thank, first, all those members of the Mashpee Wampanoag tribe who devoted time and talent to the task of explaining in detail, and with great patience, the tribe's social and political systems, kin relations, and beliefs; in particular, Randy Peters, Hannah Averett, Hazel Oakley, Joan Tavares, Kenneth and Selena Coombs, Earl Mills, Shirley Peters, Ellsworth Oakley, and John Peters. Of special note is Vernon Pocknet, whose candor and friendship were invaluable and remain so. I would also like to thank Betty Peters, who, although not a tribal member, nonetheless provided valuable insights into the controversies described in the book.

Among my academic colleagues I owe a special debt of gratitude to William A. Starna, William C. Sturtevant, Laurence Hauptman, Arlinda Locklear, and Annemarie Shimony, who read and commented on earlier drafts of the manuscript. I spent many hours in discussion of the issues embedded in this work with Starna and Sturtevant; for their valued advice and observations I am deeply appreciative, although I take full responsibility for the result. I wish also to acknowledge the contribution of the Massachusetts Council on the Arts and Humanities and the Indian Spiritual and Cultural Council for their generous support.

Finally, there is Russell Peters, who for ten years has prodded and cajoled me to complete the manuscript and who took over the responsibilities of unofficial editor, proofing and preparing the final draft for the publisher. Russell has personally paid a heavy price for the tribe's legal efforts, and it is my hope that this book, in a small way, makes amends.

Milan, New York   JACK CAMPISI
November 1990

THE MASHPEE INDIANS

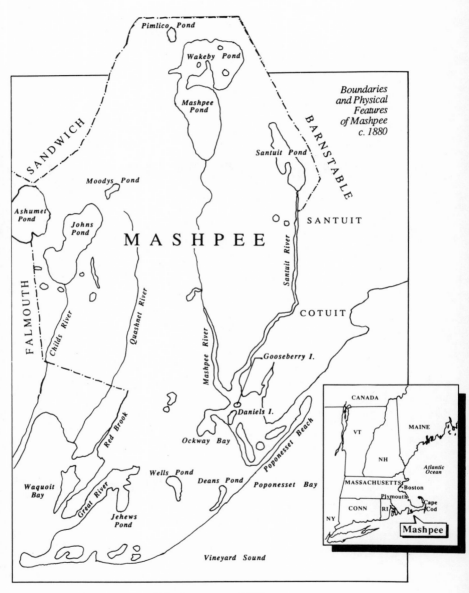

Mashpee, ca. 1880.

❖ 1 ❖

INTRODUCTION

THIS BOOK IS AN ETHNOHISTORY of a community of Indians, the Mashpees, who have occupied the same area of Cape Cod for more than 350 years of recorded time. In writing it, I have relied heavily on documents collected during the course of the tribe's suit against the town and private landholders of Mashpee, Massachusetts, a case in which I served as an expert witness. These legislative documents form a history of the group, one which is detailed and extensive but bears the mark of the English and Americans who recorded it. The memoranda, reports, legislation, and court proceedings describe the history of the tribe's relationship with the colony and the Commonwealth of Massachusetts. The Mashpees often appear incidentally in the sources and are mentioned because of their tenacious resistance to non-Indian incursions on their lands or to the imposition of unwanted outside political structures.

Despite these limitations, the documents do allow the researcher to trace Mashpee ethnohistory. In following this history, I have attempted to describe how the Mashpees have adjusted and maintained their identity despite the cultural and political changes imposed upon them from early European contact until their loss of political control of the town in the 1970s.

From the perspective of anthropological theory, this book stresses a model of ethnicity first enunciated by Fredrik Barth. According to this model, the research emphasis is placed upon "the ethnic boundary that defines the group, not the cultural stuff that it encloses" (Barth 1969:15). It is the differential behaviors between group members and those who are outside that form the social fabric which delineates ethnicity. From this point of view, the contemporary American Indian tribe is a specialized form of ethnic group. The feature that makes tribal ethnicity special, federal recognition, derives from the unique historical conditions attendant to Indian–Anglo-American relations. It is a feature of ethnicity embodied in law and affirmed and defined in countless court actions, too often in conflicting ways.

The critieria for membership in American Indian ethnic groups, tribes, do not differ significantly from those for other ethnic groups. Membership is by ascription, although as with other ethnic groups, the rule has its exceptions. Tribes consist of individuals who trace at least some of their ancestry to aboriginal populations and who recognize each other and are recognized by outsiders as Indians. They share a belief in a common ancestry, that is, membership in a group identified in the historic past; however, these groups need not have existed at the time of European contact to qualify for recognition status. In many instances, tribes were created by administrative or legislative fiat or for bureaucratic convenience. Often, a single group divided or was divided into several tribes; in other cases, a number of groups were merged into a single entity (Kroeber 1955). Nevertheless, these differences in specific tribal histories, though of great interest, do not alter the proposition that tribes may be viewed as ethnic groups, nor do they significantly affect the application of boundary maintenance theory to their study.

In at least one way, however, American Indian tribes do differ from other ethnic groups in the Western Hemisphere. All other ethnic groups have a homeland, an extracontinental base from which the émigrés derived, a people and place to which they can look for cultural roots. For American Indians the situation is strikingly different. Every tribe is, in this sense, the last line of ethnic defense. It cannot derive social and psychological support from a distant group or nation. In part because of this difference in origins, native groups share a different concept of territory. Although homeland figures heavily in the consciousness of many ethnic groups, it has a different meaning for Indians. They are recognized by virtue of their being an indigenous people. Regardless of where they presently reside, they are tied to specific territories within the hemisphere that are held or coveted by others. Because of their aboriginal status, tribes (at least in the United States) are vested with rights denied other groups. Few groups have remained on their aboriginal lands, but even those who have been moved or who have lost all land have special feelings about their aboriginal territories. The values enunciated by tribal members are couched in terms of land as a spiritual entity, not a commercial asset. Tribal histories are invariably the histories of displacement, the forced diminishment of land or its total loss. Though sadly similar, each tribe's history represents a unique aspect of its cultural history, a major part of its ethnic estate, the part to which most other aspects of tribal culture are tied.

From a theoretical point of view, the differences in legal position vis-à-vis other ethnic groups make little difference. Some tribes have been accorded special legal status by virtue of federal recognition; others have not been so honored by this serendipitous route (although they may well meet the criteria of tribes). The test is whether the group in question has sustained a viable ethnic identity over time, not whether it has been identified by act of Congress or presidential edict.

There is a second approach to the understanding of tribe, namely, the evolutionary model proposed by Elman Service and Marshall Sahlins (1958, 1960, 1966, 1968, 1971). This model asserts that societies evolve from simple sociopolitical organizations, or bands, to more complex groups, tribes, and then to chiefdoms, and eventually to states. Thus the tribe is a transitional stage and, as Morton Fried (1975) points out, little different from the band. It is the chiefdom stage, in the words of Sahlins, "that bears the weight of evolutionary advance, since it genuinely bridges a previous level of organization, the acephalous society (tribe), with the state" (1968:15). In contrast, Fried (1975) has argued that tribes, at least in North America, are not the precursors of states but rather their product. If this is so, they would fall outside this evolutionary model.

In this context, it is appropriate to mention William C. Sturtevant's cautionary note regarding evolutionary typologies. They have, in his words, "a rather ambiguous relation to the real world evidenced by archaeology, ethnohistory, ethnography, and jurisprudence" (Sturtevant 1983:3). Given our incomplete knowledge of tribal people in North America at the time of contact, it is virtually impossible to determine whether tribes preceded states or were a product of state evolution (ibid.:4). Sturtevant suggests that anthropologists stop using the term *tribe*, which has a wide range of anthropological, legal, and lay meanings, and in its stead adopt a more neutral term. He borrows the anglicized Chinese word *buluos*, meaning tribe, for the substitute (ibid.:14). I do not believe, however, that changing the terminology will necessarily simplify or clarify the research problem. The answers may be beyond our reach.

Even if Fried's theoretical modification is not accepted, the evolutionary model has little applicability to the Mashpee tribe. I do not question the general utility of the evolutionary model, but rather suggest that the social units to which *tribe* is applied are significantly different from those upon which Service and Sahlins based their model and therefore require different theoretical and analytical premises. Thus the word *tribe* does not have the same meaning in the evolutionary model as in ethnic theory.

There is yet another dimension to the question of the meaning of tribe, one alluded to earlier in this chapter. The issue of whether the Mashpee Indians, or any group of Indians, are a tribe has saliency beyond the academic. It is a legal question that affects the lives of tribal members. This question was raised in the Mashpee land suit in 1977.

To understand the critical issue in the Mashpee case, one must understand a few crucial facts about federal-Indian relations. A distinction is made between tribes with whom the federal government has acknowledged "a government-to-government" relationship and those for whom no such relationship exists. Those in the first category are said to be federally recognized tribes; those in the second, unrecognized. The federal relationship can be the result of a treaty, a statute, or an executive order. Whatever its origin, it represents an acknowledgment by the federal government of an obligation to protect tribal interests should they come in conflict with federal, state, local, or private interests.

The source of this obligation, and the one relied on by the Mashpees, is the Indian Trade and Intercourse Acts passed by Congress between 1790 and 1834. These acts prohibited the purchase of Indian land by individuals or states without the express consent of the federal government. This protection had been thought to apply only to federally recognized tribes. Because the Mashpees had no federal treaties and had never been subject to federal legislation or executive acknowledgment, the question of the applicability of the acts to the Mashpees became the critical issue in the suit.

I discuss the Mashpee case in chapters 2 and 3 with two objectives in mind. First is the issue of the legal definition of tribe. From a legal perspective, any definition of tribe is a matter of law and thus the domain of the court. It is instructive, in this context, to look at how the judge in the Mashpee case arrived at a definition and how he instructed the jury to apply it to the evidence. It is equally important to see how anthropological theory was used by the two batteries of attorneys to influence the judge in his formulation of this definition. Second (and in the same vein), I will deal, if only incidentally, with what I perceive as a number of grave problems in presenting ethnological and ethnohistorical data through the medium of trial by legal combat.

It is not my intention to present a detailed analysis of trial strategy, although such a study is a worthy undertaking. Nor is it my intent to point to heroes and villains in the scenario. I do not challenge the legal tactics of the two sides, for each had obligations to its respective clients. One of my principal concerns is the manner in which anthropological and historical data and theories were transmitted, through multiple prisms in the setting of a court, to a naive jury. In significant ways, the complexities of the case were overwhelming and the material much easier to obfuscate than to clarify. In this case, the court and jury were confused not only by the data but by the theories as well. The next two chapters describe the causes, nature, and dimensions of their bewilderment.

❖ 2 ❖

TRIBE ON TRIAL

IN OCTOBER OF 1977, the Mashpee Indians of Cape Cod entered federal court in Boston to recover land they alleged was illegally taken from them, with state acquiescence, a hundred years before. Involved in the action was a possessory claim to some thirteen thousand acres in the town of Mashpee, land that had whetted the commercial appetite of a dozen or more speculators and developers. Cape Cod, with its distinctive architecture, quaint ways, limited space, and more limited social positions, put a premium on land and attached inordinate value to its possession. By the 1960s, the Cape was opened to the benefit of the middle class, except for places reserved for, and by, wealthy and generally longtime settlers. Communities in Oyster Harbor, Wianno, Cotuit, High Grounds, Hyannisport, and others assiduously barred the doors to their private compounds, fenced and guarded their properties, and ignored the gaudy onslaught that marked much of the commercialization of the Cape. During this decade much of the Cape's available land was filled with tract housing, bungalows, motels, and a plethora of shopping malls, fast-food establishments, and restaurants. Mashpee was one of the few areas left on the Cape which had the unspoiled and ill-protected acreage needed to satisfy the desire of the nouveau riche and not so rich for their place in the American dream, or at the very least for a place proximate to it.

Mashpee underwent a precipitous growth in population in the 1960s, and the Indians, who had managed the town for a hundred years, found their power and influence diminished with each new tract of housing. The opening of Route 3, connecting the Cape to the Boston area, put Mashpee within an hour or so of the city and its environs. What had largely been a summer community with a small permanent native population soon became the new exurbia.

Not all people in Mashpee were overjoyed with this prospect and the prosperity it promised. For many, Mashpee's rural quality had been idyllic, the life pace slower and more pleasurable than the one offered by the planners and the new arrivals they enticed. The longtime residents of the town saw more than the frenetic exploitation of land and water; they saw its monopolization and the closing of a way of life. Mashpee had been a community with open access to its natural resources. Suddenly, the land was posted, the trails and ancient ways blocked by developments, game driven away by the ubiquitous builders, the waterways fouled by oil, gasoline, and septic runoff, and the beaches closed to the native community.

By the mid-1960s there were two communities in Mashpee. The Indian population was located in the northern portion of the town, and the majority of the newcomers lived in the southern end, in the area of South Cape Beach and Popponessett Bay, a tract of several thousand acres of woodland and marshes which was being drained, filled, and cleared to increase its marketability.

The contrast between the two Mashpees was striking. For the new settlers who were forced to drive through the older, poorer portions of the town to reach their development homes, old Mashpee was an embarrassment. Some talked of separating the lower portions of the town and forming their own community. There, in the south at New Seabury, along the bays and beaches, was the new Mashpee. Each house, tastefully sited on its minuscule lot, was designed as a complement to its environment and landscaped with the care devoted to an expensive coiffure. Each was provided with its protective barrier of shrubs, trees, and fences and restrictive covenants that regulated the buyer's use of the land. Of course, most new housing did not measure up to the design of New Seabury, the corporation developing the South Cape area. More commonly, the developments resembled rows of shingled boxes, each the replica of its neighbor.

The Indian portion of the town had none of the imposed symmetry of the new developments. Houses were randomly arranged, usually close to the road, the products of successive inspiration and experimentation. By and large, they were small, with attached sheds, and in need of paint and repair. Paul Brodeur, writing for the *New Yorker* magazine, gave the following description of Mashpee in 1965:

The village of Mashpee lies in the northern section of the town at the south end of Mashpee-Wakeby Pond, and is linked by several narrow, winding roads with Route 28, which parallels the shoreline of Nantucket Sound. On the day of my first visit there, I turned off onto one of these roads and drove past fifteen or twenty frame houses. Some of them were painted and others were covered with weathered cedar shingles, and most of them looked as if their occupants lived in them all year and didn't have much money; several of the back yards contained such residual clues to poverty as rusted kerosene drums, discarded refrigerators, and the stripped remains of old cars. After a mile or so, I came to a small wooden building identified by a sign: "Mashpee Post Office." Beyond, the road climbed a slight rise, and I emerged into an open area shaded by some tall elm trees, where another road entered from the left. Here, facing the juncture, stood a store with a sign that read "Ockry Trading Post." A fire station with a sagging roof and walls that were covered with curling shingles stood beside the store. I took the road to the left and drove up a hill past a modern brick school and a shack identified by a sign as the "Mashpee Library."

Diagonally across the road was a Baptist church of un-
certain age and style with shingles stained a dark, glower-
ing brown. That seemed to be the end of the settlement,
so I drove back to the juncture, pulled up before the Ockry
Trading Post, and got out. Overhead a few leaves were
drifting off the elms, and some gulls were soaring inland
on a stiff southwesterly breeze. A pair of hounds lay
snoozing by the wall of the ramshackle fire station. Except for the gulls and hounds, there wasn't a sign of life.
(1978:72)

Between Brodeur's first visit and the publication of his
article, Mashpee changed to conform more to the image evoked
by the developers. The population center shifted to the southern end of the town. The elementary school was closed and
converted into a town hall, and the former town hall was abandoned, as was the fire station. The town built a new elementary
school on the southwest side to accommodate the burgeoning
population, which, in a decade, had grown from six hundred
to more than twenty-five hundred. With this increase, the Mashpee Indians lost their ability to control their way of life. They
lost control of the Board of Selectmen, and the assessment,
zoning, and planning boards, as developers, or at least individuals sympathetic to developers, took over the policy-making
committees of the town. Ironically, in many instances, it was
the town's Indian leaders who first appointed builders to draw
up the regulations. The two dissimilar modes of living in Mashpee were in conflict, and from 1968 onward, the Mashpee Indians found they could neither prevent the one nor assure the
continuance of the other. One of the leading developers put
the matter plainly when he told Brodeur: "Our ideas reflect what
modern Americans are seeking. The Mashpees can go along
or not. It won't make any difference" (ibid.:119).

This view was not altogether accurate; the Mashpees' opinions did make a difference, but neither side could have pre-
dicted in the late 1960s the form their opposition would take.
Refusing to accept the cavalier pronouncement as inevitable,

the newly organized tribal council sought some redress in law. Actually, the resulting land suit grew out of a much smaller claim brought by the Mashpees for a share in the value of some land in Wellfleet, a neighboring town on the Cape. A routine title search had turned up evidence that some land in Wellfleet had never had titleholders and therefore was in the nature of aboriginal land. The Mashpees brought legal action to share in the benefits of the sale of the land through a nonprofit law firm, Pine Tree Legal Services, headed by Thomas N. Tureen. Tureen had gained prominence through his work in the Passamaquoddy-Penobscot land claim against the state of Maine.

There were certain broad similarities between the Maine case and the conditions of the land loss at Mashpee, and, after a series of discussions between Tureen and the leaders of the Mashpee tribal council, Pine Tree Legal Services agreed to provide legal assistance. Over the course of several months, Pine Tree provided several attorneys on a part-time basis to look into the history of the tribe's loss of the land that now constituted the town. It was at this point that Barry Margolin, a young attorney with a strong interest in advocacy, became involved. Margolin conducted an exhaustive search of the historical records to determine the conditions under which the Mashpees had lost title to and control of the land. He found that the land loss was the direct result of certain unilateral actions of the Commonwealth of Massachusetts in 1842 and 1869–70.

By these acts and others, the land, which had been held in common by the Mashpee tribe, was divided among its members, then these members were permitted to sell their holdings. A block of common land was also sold by agents of the state. Those who did not sell were subject to local taxes, and so another portion of the land was lost through tax sales. It was apparent to Margolin that soon after 1870, the year the Indian District of Mashpee was incorporated as a town, a majority of the town's land was owned by non-Mashpees. Although the acts of the commonwealth gave rise to a complaint on the part of the Mashpees, under the Massachusetts constitution there was no way to test it in court. In fact, few could even conceive of the land loss being subject to challenge; the Indians of Mashpee like other Indians in the original thirteen states were thought to be subject solely and exclusively to the dictates of the state. Nor is it at all certain that the Mashpees would have taken action had the possibility existed before the 1970s, for the effects of these legislative acts on tribal control of the town's resources were long delayed by the town's isolation. Two unrelated occurrences brought the Mashpees to court: the awareness of the peril to their way of life and the presentation of a legal means to secure a remedy.

The post–World War II period seemed hardly the opportune time for the eastern tribes to assert a federal relationship. Congress and the White House were vigorously pursuing policies to divest themselves of responsibilities to Indians, singly and collectively. Reversing the New Deal era, when Indian groups were permitted to reorganize and receive federal protection, Congress in 1953 passed a resolution establishing a national policy to "make Indians within the territorial limits of the United States subject to the same laws and entitled to the same privileges and responsibilities as are applicable to other citizens of the United States, and to grant them all the rights and prerogatives pertaining to American citizenship." To this end Congress resolved "That it is declared to be the sense of Congress that, at the earliest possible time, all of the Indian tribes and the individual members thereof . . . should be freed from Federal supervision and from all disabilities and limitations specially applicable to Indians" (U.S. House of Representatives Concurrent Resolution 108 of 1953).

This action was followed in the same year by Public Law 280, which transferred much federal jurisdiction over Indian tribes to the states (18 U.S.C.A. Sect. 1162). The Department of the Interior moved with uncharacteristic vigor to implement congressional intent. It recommended the termination of selected tribes and pressured Indians to leave the reservations and move to the cities, where they might more quickly be assimilated. These policies of termination and relocation were questioned during the Kennedy administration but were not abandoned until the first year of President Richard Nixon's term. Even then, no clearly defined alternative was put in their place, nor was there a serious challenge to the conviction that the best way to deal with Indian tribes was by eliminating them through assimilation.

Indians did not resignedly accept the federal dictates. There were protests, marches, and takeovers, some culminating in confrontations such as Wounded Knee in 1973 (Nichols 1988). In the midst of this period of policy uncertainty and growing Indian militancy, the federal judiciary opened a route for the adjudication of Indian land claims in the eastern states. In a series of decisions the courts found that the Indian Trade and Intercourse Acts of the eighteenth and nineteenth centuries applied to the original thirteen states as well as the rest of the nation and that federal protection covered equally federally recognized and nonrecognized tribes (Campisi 1985). In 1974, the United States Supreme Court held that the provisions of the Indian Trade and Intercourse Act of 1790, prohibiting states from unilaterally affecting title to Indian land, applied to the states in the Northeast (*Oneida Indian Nation* v. *County of Oneida*, 414 U.S.:661, 94 S.Ct.:772). The following year the court extended its position by holding that the act applied to any "bona fide" tribe, whether federally recognized or not, and placed a trust relationship on the federal government to protect the land of such tribes (*Joint Tribal Council of the Passamaquoddy Tribe* v. *Morton*, 388 F.Supp. 649 affirmed 528 F.2d:370).

By 1975, the elements of the Mashpees' case had taken form. The facts indicated that the Mashpees had a claim to a sizable portion of the town's land, and the decisions in Oneida and Passamaquoddy made it possible for the claim to be heard. Margolin and Tureen, acting as counsel for the Mashpees, held a series of meetings with the leaders of the recently incorporated tribal board of directors, an organization that had been formed in part as a response to their loss of political control of the town government. After much discussion, the board of directors decided it had a legitimate claim and authorized the attorneys to pursue legal action. Tribal members also discussed the possible negative effects of the lawsuit. It was decided that the attorneys should first attempt to negotiate a settlement.

The efforts at negotiation met with no success. The Mashpees' claims were not taken seriously. Finally, in the summer of 1976, the tribe filed suit for ejectment and damages against every property owner in the township. If nothing else, the action commanded the attention of the town in a way that other appeals had not.

The effect of the filing was galvanic. Protest against what was viewed as unconscionable behavior by the Indians filled the local papers. Citizens' groups formed to fight the claim. Indians were fired from town positions and defeated in town elections. There was talk of boycotting the few Indian-owned businesses and abundant threats of economic and political reprisals. Not all non-Indian residents supported these tactics; in fact, some joined together to support a negotiated settlement, but their efforts were for naught.

The selectmen of the town took steps to protect municipal interests by appropriating large sums of money for legal defense. They hired James St. Clair of the prestigious Boston law firm of Hale and Dorr to defend the town's rights. St. Clair had achieved some notoriety as one of President Nixon's attorneys during the Watergate scandal. He and his staff were joined by another team of lawyers led by Allan van Gestel of an equally prestigious law firm, Goodwin, Proctor and Hoar. This firm represented the title surety companies, which stood to lose millions of dollars should the claim be successful. Together with lawyers representing New Seabury Corporation and a few representing individual landowners, they made up an impressive, expensive collection of legal talent.

The Mashpees based their claim for recovery on the provisions of the Indian Trade and Intercourse Act of 1790, which protected the land of any Indian tribe or nation. The act, sometimes referred to as the Indian Non-Intercourse Act, provides, in part, "No purchase, grant, lease, or other conveyance of lands, or of any title or claim thereto, from any Indian nation or tribe of Indians shall be of any validity in law or equity unless the same be made by treaty or convention entered into pursuit to the Constitution" (1 Stat 137, codified as 25 U.S.C. Sect. 177).

The defendants countered that the Mashpees were not a tribe within the meaning of the statute, and therefore the law was not applicable. Thus the key legal question was, Are the Mashpees a tribe within the meaning of the act?

Throughout the winter of 1977 the sides exchanged legal salvos, briefs and counterbriefs, interrogatories, and memoranda of law. On one side were the two law firms, occupying several floors of expensive office space a few skyscrapers apart in Boston. Both were staffed with cadres of bright, ambitious young attorneys, who treated law as a joust. In the words of one observer, "Boston attorneys call each other brother and practice fratricide." Against this array was a single part-time attorney, Margolin, occupying a four-by-six-foot cubicle in a citizens' action agency.

The struggle was not restricted to legal conflict. Both sides approached national leaders for assistance. Congressman Gerry Studds and Senators Edward Brooke and Edward Kennedy took the position that they would support any compromise agreeable to both sides and then remained aloof from the controversy. Not until after the trial had commenced did the senators propose a solution; by that time it was too late (*Cape Cod Times*, Oct. 21, 1977). President Jimmy Carter sought to resolve the controversy by appointing an old friend, Judge William B. Gunter, to investigate the issues and make a recommendation for their resolution. Gunter made the grand tour of the eastern tribes, received the required ceremonial treatment — briefs and memoranda — and returned to Washington to prepare his report. Before completing it, he met with the two sides at the White House to try to get a better understanding of what the land claim was about. The Wampanoags were represented by their chief, Earl Mills, and the president of the Mashpee Wampanoag Tribal Council, Russell Peters, along with attorneys Tom Tureen and Barry Margolin. The town of Mashpee was represented by Selectmen George Benway and Kevin O'Connell and their attorney, James St. Clair. This was the first time the two sides had sat at the same table in over a year. President Carter's general counsel, Lloyd Cutler, and a representative from the Office of Management and Budget (OMB) sat in to protect the interest of the administration. It was clear that Judge Gunter did not realize the chasm that separated the opposing groups. After a few minutes of light conversation, Gunter asked how much money it would take to resolve the question. "A million, two million, or what?" Peters stated that the Mashpees were not seeking a monetary settlement. He said they wanted their land and their waters returned to the tribe to be preserved for future generations of Mashpees. The OMB representative stated that a monetary settlement could set the stage for a huge future liability for the government and that any such settlement should be viewed with caution. The selectmen, both of whom were real estate brokers, expressed concern for the non-Indian homeowners who could not buy or sell property because of the land claim. Benway said that a monetary settlement would only encourage the Indians to continue litigation. Judge Gunter declared that he was not a mediator and he would merely make a recommendation to the president. In the end, his report amounted to nothing; any federally proposed solution would have involved a federal assumption of the cost, a condition strenuously opposed by the executive's watchdogs of the budget. Gunter's solution was to let the matter go to trial (*Boston Globe*, Sept. 17, 1977).

The case proceeded toward trial before Federal District Court Judge Walter J. Skinner, a graduate of Harvard Law School and a Nixon appointee who had won high praise as a jurist. His knowledge of contemporary American Indian societies, however, verged on the nonexistent.

Judge Skinner separated the issue of tribal status from that of land title and set trial to determine the tribal question. Attorneys for the plaintiff objected, saying that this question was one to be determined by the Congress or the executive, not the courts. They pointed out that a petition for federal recognition had been filed with the Department of the Interior. When Interior would not provide the court with an assurance of a prompt determination, the judge ordered the trial to proceed. The defendants elected to have a jury trial to determine the facts in the case, and an October date was set.

After the terms of the conflict and the date for its commencement had been set by the court, the two sides began the task of preparation. By this time Tureen and Margolin had joined with a nonprofit law firm specializing in Indian land claims called the Native American Rights Fund (NARF). NARF recruited a cadre of researchers to scour the community and archives for evidence. It employed the historian James Axtell to present and interpret the historical data. This writer, an anthropologist, had a similar responsibility for the contemporary period. To give the court and jury a general understanding of the history of American Indian tribes as well as a basis for comparison, NARF brought in William C. Sturtevant, ethnologist at the Smithsonian Institution, and Vine Deloria, Jr., the noted Sioux political scientist and author. In addition, the plaintiff arranged to call to the witness stand government officials, a genealogist, and several members of the Mashpee Indian community.

The attorneys for the defendants were equally active, but in a different way. They were preparing to call only two expert witnesses: Francis Hutchins, a historian who had just completed a fellowship at the Newberry Library in Chicago, and Jeanne Guillemin, a sociologist from Boston College. Hutchins's primary responsibility was much like that of Axtell; to interpret the historical evidence. Guillemin was to conduct a survey of the Mashpees to provide evidence concerning their contemporary sociopolitical structure. She was thwarted in this effort by the almost universal refusal of the Mashpees to cooperate with her. To provide a data base, the defense attorneys took more than eighty depositions from Mashpee Indians, collecting information on a wide range of subjects including family histories, work patterns, knowledge of tribal affairs, and Indian identity. The depositions, most of which were conducted in Mashpee, took on the average three hours each to complete and required the presence of at least one of the plaintiff's attorneys, further straining the small staff. Strained, too, was the good nature of the plaintiffs, who were served subpoenas and required to answer under oath a host of questions that seemed to be invasive, meaningless, or irrelevant. In some cases witnesses were required to return several times to continue the interrogation.

As one might expect, the relations between the Indians and the majority of whites deteriorated rapidly during the summer of 1977. The selectmen, backed by an ad hoc citizens' group called the Mashpee Action Committee (MAC), took an inflexible position in opposition to the claim and effectively prevented any chance of compromise. To a lesser degree, there was a similar hardening of position among the members of the tribe.

One key element of the plaintiff's preparation for trial that remained to be determined was the selection of a trial lawyer. After considerable review and discussion, Margolin asked Lawrence D. Shubow of the firm of Shubow, Shubow, Stahlin and Bergstresser of Boston. Shubow was acknowledged to be one of the best trial lawyers in the Boston area, and he had a proclivity for taking unpopular cases. He was also a longtime summer resident of the town of Mashpee, a fact the defendants used in an effort to have him removed from the case. Almost immediately upon joining the case, Shubow found himself inundated by thousands of pages of documentation. Cast in a role somewhat unusual for him, that of an attorney for the plaintiff, Shubow had but a few weeks to work out with his younger colleague, Margolin, a strategy by which to present the complex historical record that constituted the core of the plaintiff's claim.

My first meeting with Shubow, early in July 1977, is illustrative of his style. I drove over to his camp with one of the NARF staff members late one morning and met Shubow, who had just returned from a morning swim. We sat down, and after the briefest exchange of pleasantries he began to ask questions. What did I think a tribe was? Could the Brahmins of

Boston be a tribe? Did I think that the lack of good harbors in Mashpee accounted for the Indians' long isolation? Weren't the herring runs a unique aspect of Indian life? At one point I expressed the thought that it was ridiculous to expect that a jury of twelve randomly selected citizens could decide what a tribe was when after a hundred years of study anthropologists had been unable to agree. He seemed to find that idea astounding but corrected me, pointing out that the judge would determine what a tribe was and the jury would decide whether the Mashpees met the criteria. This seemed to me as ludicrous as the first proposition, but I kept the observation to myself. I did not know at that time that the judge not only would determine the meaning of tribe but would keep secret his definition until after the trial had been completed.

The trial began on October 17 with the selection of a jury. The process was very simple: prospective jurors were called and examined by the judge. If in the opinion of the judge, the juror could render an unbiased decision, he or she was seated. In Judge Skinner's words:

> And it will be done in the following manner: The juror will be sworn and brought to the conference room adjoining the courtroom, where there will be representative counsel, not the whole platoons that we see here of lawyers, but there will be representative counsel, and I will inquire of each juror concerning matters which might affect that juror's impartiality in the case. I'll ask you, as I have before, as I know you understand, to give me the fairest and frankest answers to these questions, because the whole system depends upon an impartial jury. We are going to draw a jury of 12, even though in civil cases we commonly used a 6-person jury, and I'm drawing a jury of 12, and, I guess, 4 alternates, because of the importance of the case and the necessity to draw as large a cross section of the cross section which you as a panel represent, so that will be our procedure. (TT 1:3–4)

The judge conducted the voir dire hearing. The prospective jurors were asked their occupations, the occupations of spouses, and whether they owned land on the Cape. Could they believe a tribe of Indians, some of whom might look black or white, could still live on the Cape? Had they formed an opinion about the case, and would a long trial seriously inconvenience them? At one point in the impanelment Shubow asked the court to inquire about a prospective juror's education, but the judge refused, saying, "I think we might get into a very serious problem if the issue of education were raised, like an elitist jury" (ibid.:19). In relatively short order, the first twelve jurors were selected and each side was given three peremptory challenges. The plaintiff challenged three, the defendants two, and after these were removed, the alternates were selected. After a brief discussion between the judge and the attorneys on how to handle individuals wearing "Indian regalia" in court (the judge agreed not to permit it because it might distract members of the jury and provide an undue influence in their deliberations), the jury was seated and given some preliminary instruction by the judge.

Shubow opened the trial by defining the issue and outlining the evidence he would present. "As we understand it," Shubow told the jury, "the issue that is being carved out by the judge and being presented to you good people for determination, it's the following: Is the plaintiff a tribe today?" (TT 2:4). Shubow then proceeded to take the jury on a tour of three hundred years of Mashpee history, touching on points that would give credence to his contention that the Mashpees were a tribe. The historical review completed, Shubow categorized the nature of the evidence to be presented. In this way he also presented the jury with the plaintiff's definition of tribe. He told the jury:

> Basically, we'll be offering evidence to prove four facts. I may repeat them one more time before I am through. First, that the plaintiff is and always has been a group of Indian people: that is people of Indian ancestry, who are conscious themselves of being Indian and are recognized as Indians by the outside world.

Second, that this group of people has lived on the lands of Mashpee for hundreds of years.

Third, that the Indians on this land have made up a cohesive, permanent community with a common heritage and many, many shared ways of living, some of which carry the imprint of the past to this day, as you will hear during this trial.

And fourth, that Indian communities in Mashpee have always had their own form of organization and leadership. Sometimes it's been formal; sometimes, informal. Sometimes opposed [imposed] from the outside; and sometimes, whenever they could win the right to self-government, that leadership was chosen themselves. They've been, in other words, for 300 years — we can't prove what the situation was in 1870 without offering you evidence as to what the situation was before and what it has been since — they've been a group of Indian people living in a distinct territory in a cohesive community with their own social organization. (Ibid.:11–12)

Shubow completed his remarks with a lengthy review of the evidence that would prove his four contentions.

It was clear that the plaintiff was using as its definition of tribe one first enunciated in *Montoya* v. *United States.* In that case, the Supreme Court defined a tribe as "a body of Indians of the same or a similar race, united in a community under one leadership or government, and inhabiting a particular, though sometimes ill-defined, territory" (180 U.S. 1901:261).

Shubow's four "facts" or criteria, though not stated as concisely, hewed closely to *Montoya* in an attempt to place the weight of precedent behind the plaintiff's claim. The first criterion, that a tribe consists of a group of Indians "of the same or a similar race," though seemingly self-evident, nonetheless made it possible for a group that could not demonstrate a common ancestry to be recognized as a single entity. This was important in the Mashpee case because, as a "praying town" (a Protestant religious community), Mashpee undoubtedly included individuals from a number of Algonquian-speaking communities. The courts had consistently held that an Indian is a person who meets two qualifications: (1) at least some of his or her ancestors lived on the continent before discovery, and (2) the individual is identified as an Indian in the community in which he or she lives (Cohen 1942:2). From a practical standpoint, if this criterion were accepted, the Mashpees need only show that they were direct descendants of some group of people previously identified as Indians. Since state and federal censuses as well as birth and marriage records were available, this task was relatively easy.

  The second and third criteria required that the Mashpees be "united in a community under one leadership or government." The Mashpees contended that community was amply demonstrated by the close kin ties and the patterns of association they exhibited. "Leadership or government" implied the existence of formal structures and some centralization of power. From the perspective of the Mashpees, there was an alternative, more realistic model, one that consisted of a weak, decentralized unit which functioned on the basis of consensus. Political decisions were the result of interactions within and among the families, communicated informally to the leaders, a continuous process of exchanging information and opinions that occurred, for the most part, away from public view. Social control was maintained by the sinuous reins of gossip, ridicule, and verbal assault. Such a system virtually defied documentation. Added to the plaintiff's woes was the need to explain how the tribe continued in existence after its aboriginal antecedents had disappeared and its government structure had been repeatedly altered to fit the fancy and dictates of the commonwealth. In relying on the *Montoya* decision, the Mashpees were asserting that they should not be held to a standard of leadership or government which exceeded that present at or around the time of contact. The Supreme Court in the *Montoya* case had acknowledged this very point:

  The word "nation" as ordinarily used presupposes or implies an independence of any other sovereign power more or less absolute, an organized government, recognized officials, a system of laws, definite boundaries and the power to enter into negotiations with other nations. Those characteristics the Indians have possessed only in a limited degree. . . . As they had no established laws, no recognized method of choosing their own sovereigns by inheritance or election, no officers with defined powers, their governments in their original state were nothing more than a temporary submission to an intellectual or physical superior, who in some cases ruled with absolute authority, and in others, was recognized only so long as he was able to dominate the tribe by the qualities which originally enabled him to secure their leadership. (180 U.S. 1901:265)

The Supreme Court's argument was based on a premise that was blatantly evolutionary, if not racist, but it did support the contention of the Mashpees that they need not demonstrate a structured form of government to qualify as an Indian community.

The fourth criterion, that they occupied a particular territory, was a crucial aspect of the case because it was for the recovery of land that the case had been instituted in the first place. The Mashpees alleged that the loss of their land, which they had held in common, had been the direct result of the unilateral action of the commonwealth. Such loss could not be used as an argument to deny their existence and thus prohibit their legal action. Judge Skinner concurred with this view.

On another matter that bore heavily on the plaintiff, the judge did not concur: the matter of "burden of proof." The plaintiff contended that it was the obligation of the defendants to prove that the Mashpees were not a tribe once the Mashpees had shown that they had been a tribe. To cease being a tribe, so the argument went, they would either have had to abandon such status or have been terminated by an act of Congress. The Mashpees contended that neither condition had occurred and so they had a prima facie case for their existence, thus shifting the burden of proof to the defendant. The defendant, of course, disagreed, and so did the judge.

With the completion of Shubow's opening remarks, James St. Clair presented an outline of the defendant's position. After the usual ceremonial acknowledgments to the court, St. Clair moved quickly to the main issue of the trial; the status of the Mashpees. He told the jurors, "If I may be permitted to state what I understand the issue to be, it is substantially not whether a group of people in Mashpee consider themselves to be a community, as my brother [Shubow] had mentioned several times. The question is: Are they a tribe? Does this community exercise essential governmental functions? Is it a separate government? The defendants will show, through evidence, that under no circumstances does the community of Mashpee perform any such function" (TT 2:45).

St. Clair briefly described three factors that would support the defendants' claim. First, the federal government had never recognized the Mashpees as a tribe. Second, there had never been any taking of land from the Mashpees. Third, the Mashpees had never signed a treaty with either the Massachusetts Bay Colony, the king of England, or the United States. "So we have none of the emoluments of a formal government or state or tribe," he told the jury, "and it's for that reason we have to look back in history to see what the evolution of this group of people is, racially, economically, socially and governmentally, if you will" (ibid.:47).

Like Shubow, St. Clair took the jurors on a tour of Mashpee history, pausing only at those places which he believed supported his contention. For example, when describing Richard Bourne, a minister influential in Mashpee Indian affairs, St. Clair said:

> He conceived a group of Indians who would be Christian, who would be brought into the English system of government and would become ultimately a part and parcel of the structure of what he then believed would be an English speaking, English governed community. He conceived such a group as not being part of the Indian structure that then existed, as different. It would be English. It would be Christian. And he set about to create

such a group. And the evidence will show that the culmination of this plan on the part of Richard Bourne in 1650–1654 ultimately was realized in 1870 when Mashpee became a town, an integral part of the Commonwealth of Massachusetts its members became citizens of the Commonwealth and thereafter functioned just as any other town in the Commonwealth and not as an Indian tribe. (Ibid.:48–49)

From St. Clair's perspective, the Mashpees were not a tribe at the time of the trial, nor had they ever been a tribe. They had been a plantation, a district, and a town, and they were a community. Not only had they never been a tribe after the revolutionary period, he informed the jury, but the population did not qualify as Indians. "And, you will find the evidence rather clearly showing that there was a significant influx of other people of other racial backgrounds. So that by that point in legislation affecting the people in Mashpee, they are referred to as Indians, mulatto and black people" (ibid.:53). This transition from an Indian community to a non-Indian one was documented, according to St. Clair, by a change in religion that occurred around 1800. Richard Bourne had established an Indian church, and his successors had continued it until the 1790s, when the Baptist church was established to challenge the mission of the Congregational minister, the Reverend Gideon Hawley. According to St. Clair, "Hawley was very disturbed about the influx of black people into this community. He felt it should be kept as an Indian community and thus an Indian church. Well, the black people and their children intermarried, didn't feel too comfortable under Mr. Hawley and his church, because of his attitude toward them, so they created a church of their own, the Baptist Church where they did feel comfortable; and the tensions in the community built up between those two groups and come to a sort of a head in 1933 [sic]" (ibid.:55).

There was a logic to the approach if not the argument. If the inhabitants of Mashpee were not Indians, they could not be a tribe. If they were not Indians, what were they? Their possibly having black ancestors did not remove the possibility of their believing that they were Indians. Because self-perception was an important criterion, St. Clair felt obliged to submit evidence that they did not view themselves as Indians during the nineteenth century. "During that period of time the process of evolution continues, and it's important to see, as I view it, and the evidence will show, how the people in 1870 viewed themselves, and we're fortunate to be able to show to you the United States census for 1870. The United States census shows for 1870, that 86 and one-half percent of the people were black, and less than one-half of 1 percent were listed as Indian. We have the documents and you will see it [sic]" (ibid.:58).

What St. Clair failed to tell the jury was that the 1870 census, like those that had preceded it and those that were to follow until 1970, did not provide for self-categorization. Race was determined by the census taker from a limited list of choices. The same held true for marriage, birth, and death notices, which relied on the eye and attitude of the official.

The Mashpees, then, were a community, presumably a community of blacks, but as St. Clair informed the jury, "there is nothing wrong with being black. I'm sure the people who now claim to be Indians will agree to that. We are what we are that's not the issue. The issue is: How do we view ourselves? Separate and distinct from the rest of us in terms of government, economy and cultures? Or as part of the rest of us?" (ibid.:65). To the noted attorney, they were no more a tribe than the Italians of the north end of Boston, the Irish of South Boston, or the Jews of Brookline (ibid.:64).

St. Clair gave other reasons why the Mashpees were not a tribe. To be a tribe they had to exhibit the attributes of a domestic dependent nation, the legal enigma first proffered by Justice John Marshall in 1831. They had no courts and did not control their internal affairs, provide their own police protection, or take care of their welfare requirements. In a word, "they function as an integral part of our existing community and not as an Indian tribe" (ibid.:62). They retained none of their aboriginal culture. They spoke no language other than a regional variant of English, and their ceremonies and tribal organization were a recent development in response to the availability of federal grants, or so St. Clair asserted.

With St. Clair's completion of his opening remarks, the main work of the trial began. Before the first witness was called, however, Judge Skinner gave instructions to the jury regarding the testimony to follow. There would be two types of witnesses, he told the jurors, those who would testify to facts they had observed and those who would express opinions as expert witnesses.

> You, as I've said, are the judges of the facts. Among the facts that you are to judge are the opinions of the experts.
> If a witness is qualified as an expert, his opinion as to something that went on or the character of it becomes evidence for you, just like any other kind of evidence.
> Typically — and I think from what counsel has said, in this case as well — experts come in pairs, one on each side of the question. And you will have to make a judgement between the opinions of varying groups of experts. So keep that in mind as we hear the case that there will be experts on both sides and that it's very likely, from what I hear from the lawyers, that they will disagree. So that as you hear an expert, you consider very carefully what is said about his background, what sources he has used to form his opinion, and the basis of that opinion.
> You must keep that in mind, having in mind sooner or later there'll be another expert with a different opinion.
> With that caution, we'll take the morning recess and then proceed to the taking of testimony. (Ibid.:68–69)

The judicial caveat to the jury was well warranted. Through the opening remarks the two sides had presented significantly different criteria for the definition of *tribe*. The attorneys for the plaintiff defined *tribe* in terms of social interaction: a community of long duration, intermarried, of Indian ancestry, whose members exhibited social cohesion and were subject to social control. It was a community that for a long time had been governed under a variety of names and guises but had consistently been recognized as being Indian. Although it was not, in contemporary times, the replica of its aboriginal antecedents, such a requirement was extraneous to the question.

The defendant's attorneys took the opposite tack and argued that to be a tribe a group must exhibit a formal, well-established governmental system which exercised sovereignty and internal autonomy. Further, to be a tribe the community must be visibly Indian. It must have a language, dress, songs, and ceremonies. From the defendant's point of view, for a group to be a tribe it had to meet the criteria used to recognize tribes in 1790, the date of the controlling piece of legislation in this case. At one point St. Clair told the court that an anthropological definition of *tribe* was invalid because the science of anthropology did not exist in 1790 (TT 11:67). There was, of course, some logic to this position if anthropology is a science of invention and not discovery, as it clearly is not.

The plaintiff began presenting its case, alternating Mashpee Indians and expert witnesses. In general, the Mashpees testified about their ancestry, political organization, beliefs, and knowledge of past political leaders. They were questioned about the activities of their chief and their medicine man, the Baptist church and the tribal council, and the annual herring run and powwow. On cross-examination the defense tried to establish that the witnesses had ancestors who were black, that the tribal organization was of recent origin coinciding with the beginning of the suit, and that the tribal group performed no government functions and exercised no power over the affairs of the members.

The strategy of the plaintiff's attorneys was to present a detailed description of the convoluted history of the Mashpees and then show, by using comparative data, that there was nothing unique about this pattern, that tribes recognized by the United States were no different from the Mashpees, and that recognition was an accident of history and not the product of some special developmental process. The herculean task in all this was to move the judge and jury past their movie views of Indians and to a definition that could encompass the enormous diversities of American Indian communities. Only in that manner could the court and jury come to the opinion that the Mashpees were a tribe.

The first expert called by the plaintiff was the eminent ethnohistorian James Axtell, presently the William R. Keenan, Jr., Professor of Humanities at the College of William and Mary, who described in detail the history of the Mashpees from the early 1600s up to 1900. Axtell traced the development of the earliest community, the changes that occurred or were imposed, and the role of various missionaries. An expert on New England colonial history, he placed the Mashpees in a broad historical perspective, comparing them with other New England Indian groups. Axtell, however, addressed the definition of tribes only in an oblique and inferential manner (TT 5:2–85).

This writer, called to present data on the contemporary social organization of the Mashpees, offered the first of several definitions of *tribe*. Staying well within the parameters set by *Montoya*, I defined a tribe as a group of Indian people whose membership is by ascription, who share or claim a common territory, have a "consciousness of kind," and represent a community with a recognized leadership (TT 11:60–72). Based on these elements, I asserted that the Mashpees were a tribe.

Having described the historical and ethnographic record of the Mashpee tribe, the plaintiff presented witnesses who could show that the Mashpees' experiences were similar to those of recognized tribes in the United States, that the recognition of tribes was largely fortuitous, and that no definition that included the concepts of sovereignty or relied on racial or cultural purity or the presence of self-sustaining political and economic organizations would suffice. The first such witness called was Vine Deloria, Jr., a political scientist and member of the Sioux tribe. Margolin examined Deloria, trying to establish a definition of *tribe* and develop a broad comparative base for its implementation among American Indians. After repeated objections by the defense counsel to the content of the questions, Judge Skinner stepped in:

THE COURT: Let me try a question.

MR. MARGOLIN: Yes, your honor.

THE COURT: Can you tell us what criteria you use to identify an Indian community as a tribe?

THE WITNESS: I think . . .

MR. VAN GESTEL: Your Honor, may I politely note an objection to the question?

THE COURT: Yes.

THE WITNESS: As I use it and as I understand other Indian people using it, it means a group of people living pretty much in the same place who know who their relatives are. And I think that's the basic way we look at things. You can add or subtract all kinds of footnotes if you want, but I think that would be the generally acceptable way Indians would look at it. That's the way I look at it. (TT 17:125–26)

Margolin attempted to develop the definition by asking if there could be a tribe without a political organization. The defense objected and was overruled and Deloria was allowed to answer.

This is getting increasingly difficult to respond to, because we don't make the distinctions that you do in the Anglican [Anglo] world, religious, political, and everything else. What you are talking about is a group of people who know where they are. They may have to respond to outside pressures and adopt political structures, religious structures, or economic structures to deal with that outside society. There is no question I can answer where I have to begin to divide that community up and say we have these identifiable structures, the same way you do in the white men's world, because it's not the way I look at it. (Ibid.:127–28)

Margolin then asked if a group could be a tribe if it could not exercise political control over a territory. The defendant objected, and the judge called for a bench conference. Bench conferences are held out of earshot of the witness and jury, but they are instructive about the court's views and attitudes. This one was particularly so because it indicated that the judge either did not understand the argument made by Deloria or was opposed to it.

MR. MARGOLIN: What I'm attempting to move toward is to bring out from Mr. Deloria some of the information that he has about the characteristics of the tribes with which he is familiar.

THE COURT: It strikes me you are trying to lead him by the nose into judicial definitions, somewhat against his will, I'd say.

MR. MARGOLIN: I am not anticipating he is going to say yes, but I guess the question is — the next question would be: Are you familiar with tribes that do not or have not at some time had or exercised governmental powers?

THE COURT: Well, given his definition of tribes, the answer has got to be yes, because he said that a group is a tribe, and he says some of them don't have political organizations. It's not a single fact. So I would assume you're going to go beyond and around in circles.

MR. MARGOLIN: Well, I think that the information this witness has . . .

THE COURT: It's hard for me to understand why you are asking the question and why you are objecting, because it seems to me he (Margolin) is doing your cross-examination for you.

MR. ST. CLAIR: We may have no cross-examination.

MR. VAN GESTEL: We are getting close to that.

THE COURT: It seems to me we are going to get into — I am somewhat reluctant to have you pursue this definition, which he's given, and he's defined it, and it's plain that you see the difficulty in terms of

what I am likely to define a tribe as. You would
be advised to drop out of this and cut your losses.
But that is up to you.

MR. SHUBOW: I do think you want to know something
from him, even in the case of a tribe which already is not disputed, a federally recognized tribe,
whether they are Christian and speak English.

THE COURT: Start talking about the characteristics of
federally recognized tribes. Why don't you withdraw this question and start over again? (Ibid.:
129–30)

Margolin took the hint and commenced questioning Deloria on a variety of characteristics, attempting to show that
the Mashpees shared these in common with recognized tribes.
It is clear from the conference that Judge Skinner had formed
an opinion as to what constituted a tribe and that the broad
definition proffered by Deloria was not the direction in which
he was heading.

The plaintiff next called Jean Ludtke, an anthropologist
who had completed a dissertation on the planned community
of New Seabury (1977) and before that had written a master's
thesis on Mashpee. She became interested in the problems of
ethnic boundary maintenance and concluded that Mashpee was
an Indian community amenable to ethnic boundary research.
She spent the summer of 1973 gathering data for her thesis
and thus was familiar with the tribe's and the town's recent
history (TT 18:113–22).

Ludtke defined *tribe* as a group of people who are bio-
logically and culturally homogeneous, with strong kinship ties,
who inhabit a contiguous territory with clearly defined social
boundaries, and who recognize a leadership drawn from among
their members (ibid.:147–48). Based on these criteria, she asserted that the Mashpees are a tribe.

St. Clair handled the cross-examination. He began by
challenging Ludtke's conclusion that the Mashpees are a tribe
by referring to a passage from her thesis in which she classified

them as a band community. She had written that "an aggrega-
tion of such communities constitutes a tribe" (ibid.:159). On
this basis, St. Clair asked, was it not true that the Mashpees
were a band community and not a tribe as she contended?
Ludtke answered yes, and St. Clair then asked whether she had
changed her mind since 1973. Ludtke attempted to explain the
discrepancy between her 1973 and 1977 opinions by saying that
she had changed her mind as to the applicability of the term
tribe to the Mashpees between the writing of the first and last
chapters, but St. Clair would have none of that. He asked her
to whom she communicated this shift, and she responded, to
the attorneys for the plaintiff.

St. Clair continued to attack Ludtke's master's thesis, attempting to show that it, in reality, supported the defense's position that no tribe existed in Mashpee at the time the suit was
filed. Using an interesting technique, he read selected, damag-
ing parts of her paper, asking her to attest that he had them
read correctly. After each selection he asked a series of questions to focus the jury's attention on the issue of the quote and
any inconsistencies in the witnesses' responses. Finally, after
the better part of two days of testimony, Ludtke was excused.

Toward the end of its presentation of fact, the plaintiff
called William C. Sturtevant, ethnologist at the Smithsonian
Institution. Like others, Sturtevant was called upon to define
the term *tribe* and provide a professional opinion as to whether
he thought the Mashpees were a tribe. And, like others, he was
to present a range of ethnological data to show that other
groups recognized as tribes by the United States and the Mashpees possessed the same characteristics.

The difficulties of eliciting what at first blush seems like
relatively routine information are illustrated by an exchange
between the counsels for the plaintiff and defense and the court.
Margolin asked Sturtevant how he used the word *tribe*, and
St. Clair objected. When Judge Skinner asked Margolin if he
was asking for a definition, he answered, "No, your honor, not
exactly," which confused the judge sufficiently to necessitate
another bench conference.

THE COURT: What do you expect his answer to be to
that one?

MR. MARGOLIN: That the term tribe is a comparitive
[sic] term which requires a determination in this
case whether the characteristics of the group being studied are comparable to those of groups
who are undisputably [sic] tribes, as the term is
used, and the like. And that he relies as an ethnologist and the like and that it is not strictly a
question of definition but of methodology of figuring out whether somebody is a tribe. And that
it would proceed to a question of what factors
would he consider significant in figuring out
whether the Mashpees were a tribe, because I
think his testimony would be that.

THE COURT: I think, perhaps, it would be better to go
right to that. What factors, what are the proper
factors in the determination of whether a group is
a tribe; is that what you are trying to get at?

MR. MARGOLIN: That the factors that are significant
varied, depending on the group being studied;
that there is a group of basic relatively easy questions on which there is not any dispute in the
field. Then there is a group of disputed questions
around the edges. I am simply asking for a
definition. . . .

THE COURT: How is this going to help the jury?

MR. MARGOLIN: The ultimate purpose of the testimony
is to elicit those factors which Dr. Sturtevant believes are essential in determining whether the
Mashpees constitute a tribe in the sense comparable to that of the characteristics of other tribes
that are undisputably tribes, as recognized by
scholars in the field. (TT 21:84–87)

Judge Skinner was displeased with Margolin's line of questioning and suggested that he ask the witness how he would
determine whether a group was a tribe. Margolin agreed to use

that approach and the parties returned to their respective stations, but before they could resume testimony the defense asked for another conference. The defendant raised the issue of "bootstrapping," the practice of one expert basing an opinion on the opinion of another expert.

MR. ST. CLAIR: I'm not sure what my brother is going to do. Is he talking here in general terms? Suggesting this man has read some prior testimony and basing opinions on that, then I don't think that's appropriate.

THE COURT: His opinion is based on prior testimony in the case? I'm not going to allow it. You can't bootstrap on this. Either he is an expert because he has done some work on the subject. If his expertise depends on listening to the testimony in the case, he is in just the same position as the jury.

MR. MARGOLIN: Your Honor, Rule 703 provides that an expert could rely on that other than [what] he would normally rely on in the course of his scholarly work. In fact, Dr. Sturtevant's role as scholar is essentially as a comparative ethnologist, evaluations of essentially every tribe in the country. And if Dr. Axtell and Dr. Campisi had written manuscripts on the subject, it would be part of his routine scholarly work. (Ibid.:88–89)

Judge Skinner was unmoved by Margolin's argument, telling him, "I think it would be well advised to see what you can do, reorganize your attack. It would be a pity to have this notable gentleman here and not be able to get anything out of him" (ibid.:91). Then the judge recessed the court for lunch.

The plaintiff's case had hit a serious snag, and the lawyers spent the lunch break trying to unravel it. Sturtevant's testimony was essential to the plaintiff's argument, yet it would not be admitted if it appeared to be based on opinions expressed by Axtell and Campisi. In forming his opinion, Sturtevant could rely on facts presented by other witnesses. The problem was, in the judge's view, that there were not many facts, just "a lot of opinion."

When court reconvened, Sturtevant was asked how ethnologists determine whether a particular group is a tribe. He responded by saying that the group in question was compared with other groups recognized by anthropologists as tribes. He was asked if he had reached an opinion as to whether the Mashpees were a tribe, to which he responded affirmatively. He was then asked the basis of his opinion. Over the objection of St. Clair, he identified five factors. To be a tribe the Mashpees had to consist of a community of Indians who could trace themselves back to some common origins. They had to identify themselves and be identified by outsiders as Indians. They had to exhibit social boundaries and manifest internal social and political organization. Finally, they had to be a single, discrete social unit, neither a subdivision of a larger unit nor subdivided themselves into other units (ibid.:95–96).

One hurdle had been successfully negotiated, the criteria for determining a tribe, but another, more serious one remained. Sturtevant had not conducted any research of his own at Mashpee, and the basis for his finding remained to be determined. In response to Margolin's question concerning sources, Sturtevant responded:

A. Essentially my reading of Dr. Campisi's testimony.
Q. Was it based in any part by Dr. Campisi's own conclusions concerning whether there was a tribe in Mashpee?
A. No.
Q. Or on his conclusions as to the characteristics that you just described?
A. It's based on accepting as reasonable facts the data on these points that he presented as to Mashpee. (Ibid.:99)

After reviewing the information drawn from past testimony and used to form an opinion, Margolin asked if the Mash-

pees were a tribe. Before Sturtevant could answer, St. Clair
again objected, was overruled, and then requested a bench
conference.

Once again St. Clair raised the issue of the admissibility
of Sturtevant's opinion, arguing that it was based on conclusions and not facts. At issue was a discrepancy between the
way anthropologists work and rules of evidence. The dilemma
is summed up in the following exchange.

> MR. ST. CLAIR: It has always been the law and for sound
> reasons that you cannot bootstrap one opinion on
> another and that includes conclusions drawn
> from data. That's all Campisi did. Remember,
> you may recall, I asked, "where are your notes,"
> and all that. And I asked that they be brought,
> and they never did bring them.
>
> THE COURT: They weren't obliged to.
>
> MR. ST. CLAIR: Well it's interesting they didn't.
>
> MR. SHUBOW: You could have asked him back again.
>
> MR. ST. CLAIR: We called the day before. You should
> have made arrangements to have brought them.
>
> MR. SHUBOW: You didn't ask.
>
> MR. ST. CLAIR: I didn't ask you. I asked him.
>
> THE COURT: Gentlemen, there is more than that. Some
> technician in the field reports such and such and
> such and such. I don't think he has to submit
> notes.
>
> MR. ST. CLAIR: No. But, your Honor, there is [sic] the
> data. People can look at the data and draw differ-
> ent conclusions from it [sic]. He [Sturtevant] is
> entitled to draw his conclusions from it. Campisi
> is entitled to draw his. But he can't draw his con-
> clusions from Campisi's conclusions.
>
> THE COURT: Campisi reported some findings which were
> not conclusions, but observations. Now they may
> be inaccurate. I don't know.
>
> MR. ST. CLAIR: We are not talking about accuracy.

MR. MARGOLIN: Dr. Sturtevant has testified that those
are the kind of ethnographic observations on
which an ethnologist like himself continually relies as a scholar, and I will have him expand on
that.

THE COURT: I think it all goes to the weight of it. I
think, as I said, it is pretty frail stuff coming in
this way, but I think under the rule it is admissible. (Ibid.:104–6)

The discussion continued for some time with Judge Skinner viewing my testimony as "some ethnological or anthropological diagnosis" so as to fit it within the frame of the rule
and St. Clair voicing strong opposition. Finally, the judge, with
some reluctance, acknowledged the probative value of the
testimony and overrode the objection, telling St. Clair, "You
may have yourself a fine time marching up and down the courtroom tearing it [the testimony] apart" (ibid.:112).

This and other exchanges throughout the trial serve to
illustrate the difficulties of bringing anthropological and historical data to bear on the resolution of a legal problem. What
is fact in anthropology is not necessarily an admissible fact
in law, and what is acceptable methodology in the discipline
may well be questionable as evidence. Both the content and
its presentation are determined by rules that have other evi-
dential matters in mind. This was made clear by the difficulty
of, and controversy over, separating fact from conclusion and
in Judge Skinner's characterizations of the material as frail and
flimsy. The court and defense seemed to be looking for an ex-
perimental model with its implication of replicability. The rules
of evidence are designed to ensure that the jury hears facts or
opinions based on facts; however, facts in anthropology are
sometimes the recorded observations of the fieldworker, who
exercises no control over variables and who stresses the ano-
nymity of the sources. With a researcher's field notes, another
researcher should come to the same or at least a similar conclusion, assuming agreement on definitions, which certainly

was not possible in this instance. In fact, another fieldworker should get the same results independently, but, as we shall see, this was attempted and failed.

With the epistemological questions out of the way for the time being, Sturtevant resumed his testimony. Having established that the witness believed that the Mashpees were a tribe, Margolin next sought to show that the tribe's history and development were similar to those of federally recognized tribes. He asked Sturtevant if there were any tribes that emerged after European contact (Seminole tribe of Florida and Miccosukee tribe of Florida); were any created in the recent past (Seneca-Cayuga tribe of Oklahoma in the 1930s); did any adopt Western forms of political organization before the Indian Reorganization Act (Creek, Cherokee, Seneca Nation of New York); were any of the tribes Christian (a majority, including the Oneidas of Wisconsin, Stockbridge in Wisconsin, Tuscaroras in New York); and were there tribes that spoke English exclusively (Quapaw, Wyandot, Chumash, Catawba, Miami, Lipan-Apache). Margolin finished the questioning for the day by showing, through the witness, that in the federal censuses up to 1970, the census taker determined the interviewee's race.

Sturtevant returned to the stand the next day, the twenty-second day of the trial, to testify further on the meaning of *tribe*. He described, through questioning, another usage of the term *tribe*. Certain scholars such as Elman Service used the term to distinguish one of several stages of social evolution: band, tribe, chiefdom, and state. Such a scheme, Sturtevant told the court, tended to treat the groups as though they had no history. As a result, one of the leading theorists in this area, Morton Fried, took the position that there were no tribes, that is, groups whose organization had not been strongly influenced by nations. These groups he called "secondary tribes" (TT 22:4–5).

To reinforce the distinction between the two concepts of tribe, Sturtevant read to the court a statement by Alfred Kroeber, "perhaps the leading anthropologist specialist on North American Indians" (ibid.:7), quoted in Fried's article "The Notion of Tribe" (1975).

The more we review aboriginal America, the less certain does any consistently recurring phenomenon become that matches with our usual conventional concept of tribe; and the more largely does this concept appear to be a White man's creation of convenience for talking about Indians, negotiating with them, administering them — and finally impressed upon their own thinking by our sheer weight. It cannot yet be fairly affirmed that the current concept of tribe is wholly that. But it certainly is that in great part, and the time may come to examine whether it is not overwhelmingly such a construct. (Ibid.)

Sturtevant then provided the court with an analysis of the impact of European contact on tribal organization.

So there, Kroeber is making a similar type of distinction between our usual conventional concept of tribes, that being sort of a social theory discourse as opposed to the real nature of tribe as a result of the impingement of European societies, which implies that the effects of Indians having to deal with European settlers and European military forces and European economy, there is also an effect, and the usual effect, frequent effect is to result in a greater centralization, social and political centralization. Europeans consistently say that Indians, in effect, must have a leader, and if they haven't got a leader, they damn well have to find one, or the Europeans will find one, appoint one, and deal with that person and start passing out goods to him or rights to him or demanding things, demanding that he hold his populace to account.

So in this kind of way, it's fairly easy to see how a more centralized, more powerful political system results in the course of having to defend themselves against whites.

In a military way and in other ways, it's clearly rational to cooperate among themselves more frequently, and more systematically in order to erect a barrier against the impinging white society so that the result is to incr' ase boundaries, increase political organization internally, and in the course of settlement, as non-Indians moved into the territory they begin occupying part of the territory, and Indians are pushed together in groups, filling in the territory so that they become more nucleated, they become islands, as it were, in a sea of non-Indians. (Ibid.: 7–9)

According to Sturtevant, no American Indian society has been able to survive without taking into account the pervasive influence of non-Indian societies (ibid.:10). Thus we should not expect to find aboriginal forms extant. That every Indian tribe reflects modifications in its institutions because of Euro-American influences does not mean that they are no longer tribes. Here, Sturtevant made a distinction between acculturation and assimilation. He defined *acculturation* as the adoption by one group of the cultural traits of another, "a borrowing of customs." In contrast, *assimilation* means that the members of one group have been incorporated with the body of another; the group ceases to exist as a separate social entity. He explained to the court:

> If you apply it to individuals, those two concepts, then an acculturated Indian, in shorthand form, an Indian who most of his cultural traits are of historically non-Indian origin, that says nothing about his membership in a social group, a tribe. An assimilated Indian is an Indian who has left his Indian tribe, his Indian society, and has joined and been accepted by some other society, in this case, the larger non-Indian society.
>
> Q. Has acculturation taken place among some American Indian tribes?
> A. It's taken place among all American tribes.
> Q. Including Mashpee?
> A. Including Mashpee.
> Q. Has assimilation taken place among American Indian tribes?
> A. Assimilation of individuals has probably taken

place among all; but assimilation of whole tribes, no. Those that survive are not assimilated, or are only minimally assimilated.

Q. What is the effect of [ac]culturation on the Mashpee status as a tribe?

A. No effect on their status as a tribe.

It may well affect, it has affected the cultural symbols that I used to identify the Mashpees as a tribe. Those symbols may be, some of them are, borrowed from non-Mashpee sources or in another way chosen from traditional Mashpee sources but chosen under the influence of the larger society. So, for example, I think that one could make a case for the powwow as a particular Mashpee custom and a symbol of Mashpeeness as in part a culture [an acculturative] phenomenon. The term itself "powwow" goes back to New England Algonqui[a]n language, although its meaning in aboriginal times was quite different from what it is now.

The form of the Mashpee powwow, as I understand it, is very like the form of other powwows in other Indian tribes, and powwows are something that both Indians and non-Indians expect Indians to do as Indians.

Q. Is there a sense in which Mashpee, the Mashpee are nonassimilated?

A. The sense that the Mashpee are a tribe as the Mashpee are not assimilated.

Q. What does that mean?

A. That's the feature of them being a bonded [bounded] social group, them being set off from the rest of society by social boundaries, and the rest of the country by fairly, by easily identifiable social boundaries in terms of interaction, in terms of resident [residence] patterns, in terms of self-identification and identity [identification] by the larger society.

Q. Does it matter to you as an ethnologist how [ac]culturated a group is?

A. It is an extremely interesting ethnological phenomenon, yes.

Q. But in terms of whether the group is a tribe?

A. No, there it matters not.

Q. Are there other tribes which are essentially as
[ac]culturated as Mashpee?

A. Yes.

Q. And are those groups which are universally acknowledged as tribes?

A. Yes. (Ibid.:27–29)

St. Clair conducted the cross-examination of Sturtevant,
covering a wide range of subjects but always directed toward
demonstrating that the witness had no special knowledge of
the Mashpees, had relied on insufficient information in forming his opinions, and had an inadequate or at least imprecise
understanding of the word *tribe.* At times the exchanges were
sharp and confrontational.

Q. Now, sir, when you have used the word "tribe" in
this case, you have not used that word in any legal
sense, have you?

A. I'm not a lawyer, I don't know the legal sense.

Q. The answer, then, I take it, is you have not purported to use the word "tribe" in any legal sense.

A. Purported, no, I have not purported.

Q. Now, I take it that the word "tribe" in the anthropological sense that you have used the word does
not have a precise meaning, so far as you as were
concerned?

A. I believe I used it in several anthropological senses.

Q. Do you have, when you testify in this courtroom, a
precise definition for the word "tribe," a single
definition?

A. Yes.

Q. Would you tell us what that definition is, sir?

A. The easiest way would be to have read back what I
    said yesterday. I can try to reproduce it again.
        It's a group that is descended from aboriginal In-
    dian[s]; that is a bounded social group—that is
    summarizing what I said—has recognized identity
    as Indian, recognized by themselves and by their
    neighbors; has groupwide internal social and politi-
    cal organizations; does not have any subdivisions
    which are more like tribes elsewhere than that divi-
    sion itself; nor does [is] it a part itself of a larger
    group which is more like tribes elsewhere than that
    group is.

Q. Now, in addition to that definition, as I understand
    it, you have used the word in the comparitive [sic]
    sense?

A. In the theoretical sense. This definition itself is in
    part comparitive [sic].

Q. I was going to ask you that.
        When you say it is, let's say, a bounded social
    group, you mean, if I understand your testimony
    correctly, compared to other recognized tribes?

A. In part, but also compared to the social groups
    with which it shares boundaries.

Q. But it's a comparison. There is no absolute stan-
    dard in your definition.

A. The meaning of the word depends on the other—
    the other cases to which it's been applied in effect.

Q. Most of the cases to which it's been applied are so-
    called recognized tribes, are they not?

A. Bounded social group?

Q. As tribes.

A. Excuse me?

Q. I'll withdraw the question if you don't understand.

A. Better try another one. (Ibid.:43–45)

The testimony continued in this vein for the better part
of a day, after which the plaintiff rested and the defense presented its case.

The burden of presenting the defendant's argument that the Mashpees were not a tribe fell to Jeanne Guillemin, a sociologist from Boston College. To study the Mashpees, Guillemin developed a survey to be given to a randomly selected group of tribal members whose names had been drawn from the tribal membership list. In all, she selected fifty-four persons from a list of approximately seven hundred (ibid.:27:110). But Guillemin's efforts to survey the Mashpees ran into a serious obstacle; with but two exceptions, the Mashpees she contacted refused to speak to her. Stymied, the defense attorneys came up with a novel solution. They issued subpoenas to fifty-eight Mashpees selected by Guillemin, who, under oath, responded to questions asked them by the defendant's attorneys. Guillemin made recommendations as to content, but the questions were drawn up by the lawyers. From this body of data (the fifty-eight depositions), Guillemin developed a statistical analysis upon which, in part, she based her opinions about the Mashpees. The methodology was unorthodox and resulted in an extended voir dire over the validity of the study. In the end, the defense decided not to present the data, although the witness used the findings as a basis for her opinion.

In addition, Guillemin had the responsibility of defining for the defense the meaning of *tribe*. The parameters of that definition had been laid out by St. Clair in his opening remarks, and it was thus up to the witness to provide substance and detail. For her definition Guillemin relied on the works of two noted American anthropologists, George Murdock and Julian Steward. The testimony, with St. Clair questioning, went as follows.

Q. Would you tell us in substance what first Dr. Murdock's definition of the tribe and then Dr. Stewart's [Steward's]?

A. The basis for a definition of a tribe that George Murdock used emphasizes the sovereignty of a particular group; that is, a tribe is known by, and I quote here, "original and definitive jurisdiction over

some sphere of social life in which the organization
(tribe) has the legitimate right to make decisions
having a significant effect on its members." It gives,
as an example, the allocation of economic resources,
punishments of legal infractions, control of labor,
et cetera.

Q. Is Dr. Murdock's definition recognized by anthropologists as being an authoritative definition?

A. Yes, it is.

Q. Now will you outline for us Dr. Stewart's [Stew-
ard's] definition?

A. Dr. Stewart's [Steward's] definition deals more with
cultural aspects of tribal organization. He relies on
three characteristics. The first one is basically the
sovereignty one, that is, that a tribal group is fairly
simply organized and independent and self-con-
tained and with that is the understanding that it's
usually a fairly isolated group. The second aspect
has to do with cultural uniformity.

Q. Cultural what?

A. Uniformity. Unity. Uniformity. The idea that most
people in the community conform in terms of their
values and behavior to a certain general standard.
It's acceptable by everyone. The third characteristic
is that the culture of the tribe is unique relative to
other cultural traditions. Those are the three aspects. (TT 31:110–11)

Using these criteria, Guillemin concluded that the Mashpees
were not a tribe.

The cross-examination of Guillemin was extensive, detailed, and at times acrimonious. She was questioned on her
knowledge of the Mashpees, her methodology, and her definition of *tribe*. Under cross-examination she acknowledged that
neither of the writers upon whom she relied for her definition used the term *sovereignty* in his definition. Shubow, who
handled the cross-examination for the plaintiff, returned repeatedly to the witness's definition. Finally, at the request of
the court, Guillemin read the portion of Steward's work that

she used to formulate her definition. Though admitting that the quote did not contain the troublesome word, she maintained that it was implied.

Shubow was far from done. This time he targeted on the Murdock definition.

> Q. You will remember that in Court you gave the words in quotes: "Original and definitive jurisdiction over some sphere of social life in which the organization (tribe) has the legitimate right to make decisions having a significant effect on its members," and then you went on and gave some examples. It gives as an example the allocation of economic resources, punishments of legal infractions, control of labor, and so forth. I now read to you from the Ethnology V. 1, 1962, pages 265–286, Ethnographic Atlas headed column 32: Jurisdictional Hierarchy. (TT 34:32–33)

Shubow then read a passage from an article entitled "Ethnographic Atlas," which Guillemin acknowledged was the source of the Murdock definition she used and quoted to the court:

> "This column is derived from the codes on the number and typology of 'sovereign organizations' with which Swanson obtained highly illuminating results in his study of religion. Our definition of jurisdictional levels coincides closely with his definition of organization characterized by sovereignty, i.e., by original and definitive jurisdiction over some sphere of social life in which the organization has the legitimate right to make decisions having a significant effect on its members, e.g. distribution of food, allocation of productive resources, punishments of delicts, assignment or conscription of labor, levying of taxes, initiation of war or peace."

> Q. Isn't that what you gave in this court as the Murdock definition of a tribe?

> A. Yes, it is.

Q. Does Murdock use the word "tribe" in that definition I've just read to you?

A. Not in this particular source.

Q. Who inserted the word "tribe" within those
   quotations?

A. Actually, John Whiting did it and I took the liberty
   of doing it here.

Q. You read a quotation in this courtroom from Murdock and specifically said quote, unquote, and inserted in that quotation the word "tribe" without
   letting us know it was not part of the quotation?

A. It was part of the prior discussion, not in this particular source, but in another —

Q. Dr. Guillemin, you didn't tell us that yesterday, did
   you?

A. No, I read directly from my notes, parenthesis,
   tribe.

Q. Do you remember my question Dr. Guillemin
   about the Murdock definition, "you were quoting
   from something, I think?"

A. Yes.

Q. You didn't tell us you'd made an addition to that
   quotation, namely, the word "tribe"? (Ibid.:33–34)

Shubow finished by asking the witness if she had not
made an effort, after agreeing to serve as a witness, to find a
definition of *tribe* that included the word *sovereignty*, and,
not finding one "you went and found a definition of the word
'sovereignty' and added the word tribe." The defense objection
was overruled and the witness allowed to respond. She said,
"No." With this Shubow moved to strike all portions of the
testimony having to do with the "notion of tribe," but the judge
denied the motion, saying it was for the jury to sort out.

The last expert witness for the defense was Francis Hutchins. His direct testimony covered three days and consisted of
a detailed review of the historical records, from which he concluded that the Mashpees had not been a tribe at any time from

1666 through 1976 (TT 36:141). He defined a tribe as "an entity composed of persons of American Indian descent, which entity possesses distinct political, legal, cultural attributes, which attributes have descended directly from aboriginal precursors" (ibid.:124). By political, he told the court, he meant that there was present an acknowledged leadership and a structure for decision making accepted by the members of the group and based on an internal organization different from that "followed by the ordinary citizens of the United States" (ibid.:126).

Hutchins spent the next two days under cross-examination defending his definition and historical interpretations. While steadfastly maintaining that the Mashpees had never been a tribe, he did acknowledge under questioning from the court that there had been a tribe called the Cotachessett in Mashpee in the first half of the seventeenth century and that tribe had as its leaders some of the same people who had received land under the name of the South Sea Indians (TT 37:117).

By the time Hutchins left the witness stand, the trial had produced a bewildering variety of definitions of tribe, more than the judge could take or the jury could fathom. With but a few days left in the trial, Skinner called the lawyers to the side bar and announced:

> THE COURT: I am seriously considering striking all of the definitions given by all of the experts of a tribe and all of their opinions as to whether or not the inhabitants of Mashpee at any time could constitute a tribe. I let it all in on the theory that there was a professionally accepted definition of tribe within these various disciplines. It is becoming more and more apparent that each definition is highly subjective and idiosyncratic and generated for a particular purpose not necessarily having anything to do with the Non-Intercourse Act of 1790, and I am rather persuaded that it is doing, rather than helping us, it is simply making the issue more difficult. I certainly invite comments. (TT 36:189–90)

Van Gestel spoke first, arguing that a number of definitions were used by the disciplines and about all that could be expected was that they be given a hearing. Skinner countered that not only was there no accepted definition in history or anthropology, but, worse, "You figure that whatever definition of tribe you want, you just go find the right anthropologist, and you can get it" (Ibid.:190). Shubow suggested that since the court was going to instruct the jury as to the meaning of *tribe*, it would be valuable for the jurors to keep in mind how closely the experts' definitions were to the judge's. But Skinner seemed not to be listening. "As long as they [experts] stay with their thing," he told the lawyers, "they are in pretty good shape. It is when we get into these grandiose definitions that they all seem to be in trouble" (ibid.:193). The conversation meandered on a bit longer with the attorneys bickering over the quality of the ongoing testimony and the judge musing about the possibility of cutting "some new ground," presumably meaning establishing a new legal definition of *tribe*. Finally, after thirty-eight days of trial, the two sides rested.

The trial had begun to answer a deceptively simple question: Are the Mashpees a tribe within the meaning of the Non-Intercourse Acts? This, in turn, required a definition of *tribe* and the ascertaining of facts. But without an agreed-upon definition either in law or in social science, the search became a matter of fielder's choice. The sides presented witnesses whose definitions were consonant with their legal arguments. This portion of the trial was geared to influence the judge in the formation of his definition; however, in the end the conflicting views led him to discount all the alternatives for one of his own creation, one founded on less substance than those he discarded.

The jury was charged with the determination of fact. But this was not simply a matter of determining which set of experts was telling the truth because the experts were testifying to more than the events. They were speaking of their significance as indicators of tribal identity. No one questioned that a deed existed granting a group of Indians called the South Sea Indians the land in Mashpee. The question was, Did this demonstrate the presence of a tribe? Definition and analysis were inseparably linked. The question of whether the Mashpees were a tribe depended on the definition used. By not accepting the existing legal definition or offering one of his own at the onset, the judge subjected the jury to three months of confusing, conflicting, and sometimes unintelligible testimony.

Two chores remained, summation by the opposing attorneys and the charging of the jury by the judge. St. Clair stressed two points, the triracial quality of the Mashpees, which, he asserted, gave them a questionable claim to being Indian, and the lack of evidence of strong and continuous leadership. The Mashpees were not a tribe, nor had they ever been one. Until very recently they had not thought of themselves as a tribe, at least not in 1870 when they became a town, and they did not exhibit the trappings of a tribe. Their chief was an honorary titleholder without power and with little influence, their high level of intermarriage was not unique for a small isolated community, and their cultural identity, he scornfully argued, was restricted to a few recipes.

Shubow responded in his turn that the Mashpees met all the criteria of a tribe and the problem of understanding this was related not to the Mashpees but to American stereotypes of Indians, which are based on patently false assumptions. The concept of tribes was an English idea, he told the jury, which did not come into use until the mid-eighteenth century. Historically, Indian groups including the Mashpees had exhibited weak, decentralized leadership. The defense had made a veiled appeal to racism, which should be ignored. What was worth noting, he told the jury, was the determination with which this tribe had survived 350 years of pressure to assimilate. He urged the jury not to rob them of their identity.

It was now Judge Skinner's turn to instruct the jury. He began by describing to them the nature of the facts they were to find. First, they must decide if the Mashpees were a tribe on any of five specific dates, beginning with July 22, 1790, the date of the first Non-Intercourse Act, and ending with May 28, 1870, the date of their incorporation as a town. Second, they had to determine if the Mashpees were a tribe on August 26, 1976, the date of the commencement of the suit. Third, the judge told them, "If you find that other people living in Mashpee constituted an Indian tribe or nation on any of the dates prior to August 26, 1976, listed in Special Question No. 1, did they continuously exist as such a tribe from such date or dates up to and including August 26, 1976?" (TT 40:6). In other words, the jury had to find a continuous tribal existence from 1790 onward to find for the plaintiff. In determining these facts, the burden of proof was on the plaintiff. "What this means," he told the jurors, "is that if you are left in doubt as to a particular issue that is material, you must find for the defendant or give a negative answer to the question, if you find that there is a gap in the evidence, that you don't have enough to go on, that is the plaintiff's problem, and you must answer it negatively" (ibid.:8–9). Skinner then proceeded to summarize in the briefest manner the testimony of each witness.

It was now time for Judge Skinner to "break new ground," to tell the jury his definition of *tribe*. Lecturing extemporaneously, he gave a cursory background on the legal history of the term and then stated the definition from the *Montoya* case: "a body of Indians of the same or a similar race united in a community under one leadership or government and inhabiting a particular though sometimes ill-defined territory" (ibid.: 36). The difficult task, according to the judge, was in applying the general rule to the evidence, and to that end, he offered a series of amplifications of the definition's component parts. The first of these related to the question of whether the Mashpees were Indians. It was clear from the testimony, he told them, that both plaintiff's and defendant's witnesses agreed there were Indians in Mashpee in the 1660s and that these Indians shared a common culture and language. Later, there was an influx of non-Indians who intermarried with the Mashpees, a perfectly natural phenomenon, he said. The question was, Were they absorbed into or had they radically altered the Indian society? "You must then decide whether this influx of outsiders was such as to change the character of the group from an Indian group to a mixed group, so mixed that it could not be fairly considered, all other things being equal, as an Indian tribe" (ibid.: 38–39). The statement was specious and at odds with the generally accepted definition of an Indian as a person, some of whose "ancestors lived in America before its discovery" and who "is considered an Indian by the community in which he lives" (Cohen 1942:2). Skinner, in departing from the two criteria given by Cohen and introducing the idea that the degree of mixing was the controlling factor, gave credence to the racial arguments made by St. Clair.

On the second criterion, that they be "united in a community," Skinner emphasized that there had to be social boundaries that separated the Mashpees from the neighboring communities. They had to be perceived as an Indian community and not as a community of Indians. It did not matter that the social boundaries were the result of white discrimination, but, he cautioned them, "If you remain unsatisfied of the scarcity or dearth of evidence on the point, well, then, the plaintiff fails with respect to this element of the tribal existence during this period, but you are free to draw inferences and to consider all of the circumstances on that point" (TT 40:40).

The territorial element, the third component of the definition, was "relatively clear," according to the court. The Mashpees held title collectively with an entailment on the land which prohibited individuals from selling portions to nonmembers. This condition persisted until 1842, when the entailment was removed. In 1869, the restriction against the sale to outsiders was lifted by the state legislature. The Mashpees' land title had been described by witnesses in two ways, as a proprietorship and as a plantation. A proprietorship was a land company, a self-liquidating corporation, while an Indian plantation was to continue in perpetuity.

> So that there was a very critical difference. The proprietorship was ultimately self-liquidating. The plantation at Mashpee was to continue as a plantation, so far as can be determined, in perpetuity. So that the label given to

> it as a proprietorship may be accurate in some respects
> and clearly not in others. Now, the question for you to
> decide is whether in accepting this property, accepting
> these rights with their limitations, the Indians intended
> to give up their tribal organization, or whether it was
> simply the tribal organization carrying on as owners of
> this plantation with a different label. (Ibid.:44–45)

In making this distinction, however erudite it might seem,
the judge ignored that both systems were imposed on the Mashpees to serve the conveniences of the Crown and commonwealth.
The court created a false and meaningless dichotomy and provided the jury with a spurious but important distinction from
which it could imply tribal abandonment.

There remained the issue of leadership or government in
the context of this trial. On one hand, he told the jury, there
is not much evidence of regulation; on the other, there may
not have been much need for it with only a few hundred people, grouped in a few families and occupying some thirteen thousand acres of land. The amount of government and the type
or quality of leadership were matters for the jury to determine.
He informed them, however, that leadership could not be spo-
radic or of the ephemeral type that occurs only during times
of crisis (ibid.:47). Sovereignty was not an issue because it was
not a defining characteristic of a tribe or essential to tribal leadership. Contradicting himself, Judge Skinner went on to tell the
jury that as a necessary element of tribal existence, leadership
had to have evolved from "a once sovereign Indian community" (ibid.:49–50). The leadership could take different forms
at different times, but there had to be continuity traceable to
an aboriginal antecedent.

Once the jurors had applied the four criteria — race, territory, community, and leadership — to the period before 1900,
they then had to apply them to the contemporary group. They
would not find a land base in the ordinary sense because that
was the matter of the complaint. But to find for the plaintiff,
the jury had to be convinced of the existence of a separate com-

munity made up of people of Indian ancestry, who recognized "there was controlling leadership of significant elements in the lives of the people" (ibid.:59). In addition, that leadership must be supported by a majority of the population.

The judge instructed the jury for over three hours. It took the attorneys another two hours to make known their objections, most of which Skinner rejected. But one objection raised by St. Clair was not easily brushed aside. At one point in his instructions, Skinner had indicated that a nontribal group could have evolved into a tribe, while at another point he indicated that as a requirement for tribal existence there had to be a demonstrated connection with a preexisting sovereign tribe. Skinner acknowledged the inconsistency, then told the lawyers: "But I don't think I'm going to change it even so. I suggest it's just one of those messy descriptions of the human condition that I was talking about" (ibid.:107). A day later, however, the judge changed his mind and called the jury from its deliberations to instruct it further on this contradiction. He said, in essence, that there could have been a tribe in the area he called the Cotachessett, who "were run by a committee of sorts" and that "committee" assumed control of the land in Mashpee and, in time, the inhabitants of this land "acquired the characteristics of a tribe" (TT 41:3). It would seem that there is no limit to the agility of the legal mind.

The judge's charge presented something for everybody. It gave the plaintiff the basic definition it had sought but modified it enough at least minimally to satisfy the defendant. But the judge went well beyond the effort to satisfy the parties; he altered the definition sufficiently to affect the outcome. It seems clear from his comments that Skinner could not accept the possible consequences of the application of the Non-Intercourse Acts in this case and because he could not control the facts, he changed the rules by which the facts were to be judged. He made his views explicit when he told the attorneys:

> I think that you have got a constitutional question, really. You (Margolin) are saying that somebody who sells his

land in 1842 fully and freely and for fair consideration with full knowledge, and being otherwise an adult human and so on, can get it back just for the say so 150 years later, and that rather severely distinguishes that group from the rest of the population; and, if you are going to make that distinction as a constitutional question, you have to show that there is a real honest-to-God difference between that group and everybody else; *and, you know the remedy you are seeking is a very radical remedy. It seems to me quite proper to say that whoever seeks that remedy has got to show that they are in a radically different kind of status than other people.* (TT 38:190–91; emphasis added)

Although it was reasonable to set standards that differentiated between Indian tribes and other groups in society, it was not reasonable to draw those standards in such a way as to make them unattainable even for federally recognized tribes, which is precisely what Judge Skinner proposed to do. While acknowledging that there was no single set of criteria all tribes could meet and that federal tribal status was serendipitous, the judge then proceeded to draw his own definition, which few could meet. The radical remedy for taking Indian land was imposed by the federal courts not to protect the Indians as much as to ensure federal preeminence in the field of Indian relations. Skinner was trapped by his own legal prejudices. He could do no less than define away the plaintiff.

❖ 3 ❖

A TRIBE FOR OTHER PURPOSES

T HE JURY received the Mashpee case on January 4, 1978, and, after two days of deliberation, returned its verdict. In the course of his lengthy instructions, Judge Skinner had provided the jury with six questions. To decide for the plaintiff the jury had to find that the Mashpees were a tribe on each of six dates chosen by the judge and that they had been a tribe in continuous existence since at least 1790. If the jury answered no on even a single date, it had to answer no on all subsequent dates, for to find that the Mashpees were not a tribe at one time but were at a later time would be tantamount to the jury creating a tribe.

The jury's findings were confusing, but in this they were consistent with the trial and the judge's instructions. To the question of whether the Mashpees constituted a tribe in 1790, the jury answered no; but the jury then found that they were a tribe in 1834 and 1842, but not a tribe in 1869 and 1870. Finally, the jury determined that the Mashpees were not a tribe in 1976 and had not been a tribe continuously since at least 1790 (447 F. Supp. 940 [1979]: 943).

The attorneys for the plaintiff immediately filed objections to the jury's findings claiming, among other points, that they were fatally flawed and inconsistent with the instructions. Judge Skinner took these and other objections raised by the two sides under advisement.

While the parties waited for the judge's final order, the plaintiff's attorneys found out by accident that one of the jurors had received an anonymous call in which the caller had told the juror, "You know which way you better go" (592 F:2d 575 1979:592–93). The juror had related the incident to other individuals who were traveling on the same commuter bus from Cape Cod to Boston. Margolin and Shubow immediately brought the information to the attention of Judge Skinner, who informed the attorneys for the defendants. He then called in the individual who had overheard the juror's conversation. Under oath, the witness repeated his statements and further asserted that, on occasion, the juror had discussed aspects of the trial with fellow passengers. Based on this information, Skinner called in the juror, who admitted that he had received the call but denied holding any conversations regarding the trial. The plaintiff's attorneys sought to expand the inquiry into several related areas, but the judge refused permission. He did allow a question as to whether other jurors had reported similar calls, to which the juror answered in the negative. This question brought a strong protest from the defense attorneys, and the judge refused permission to continue questioning. At least two questions that seemed germane remained unasked: had the juror told other jurors about the call, and what did the juror think the call meant—what way would be the better way to go? The judge, having satisfied himself, closed the proceeding and gagged the respective counsels.

On March 24, 1978, Judge Skinner issued his "Memorandum and Order for Judgement." In it he briefly reviewed his theory of the nature of the Mashpee tribe and, after that perfunctory introduction, turned to the objections raised by the plaintiff. The first objection related to the alleged inconsistencies in the responses, which suggested confusion on the part of the jury concerning the instructions. Skinner summarized the two parts of the plaintiff's objection:

1. There was no material change in the circumstances of the Mashpee proprietors between 1842 and 1869 which

warrants the jury's finding that they were a tribe in 1842 and were not in 1869. Since I had instructed the jury that tribal status once abandoned could not be regained, the mistake with reference to 1869 required a negative answer with respect to 1976. Thus the answer with respect to 1976 cannot be the basis of a judgement adverse to the plaintiff.

2. The finding of the jury that the proprietors were not a tribe in 1790 is inconsistent with the finding that they were a tribe in 1834. Plaintiff claims that the instructions limited the time for the emergence of a tribe to the period before 1723. The proprietors would not therefore have become a tribe between 1790 and 1834. The finding thus reflects either a misunderstanding of the instructions, or a refusal by the jury to bide by them, either of which vitiates all of the jury's answers including the answer that the plaintiff was not a tribe when the suit was commenced in 1976. (447 F. Supp. 940 [1978]:948)

Skinner disposed of the first objection by suggesting that it was arguable, on the basis of the evidence, that between 1842 and 1869 "the proprietors had reoriented their efforts toward assimilation into the general non-Indian community" (ibid.:949). This finding, Skinner went on, was justifiable because of the absence of any expression of self-identification as Indians and because of the failure of the group to establish common lands after 1869. One wonders how they might have accomplished the latter given that the state had acted unilaterally in the same period to sell the lands the tribe held in common.

It is difficult to discern precisely what evidence the judge and jury found so compelling. The basic division of tribal land had occurred in 1842, when judge and jury recognized that a tribe existed, but in 1869 the Mashpees supported the right to alienate land, although by no means unanimously. It is doubtful whether their agreement was necessary. The state's intentions were manifestly clear, "civilizing" the Mashpees, and state action was merely the forerunner of national policy — the General Allotment (Dawes) Act of 1887. On the issue of citizenship, the Mashpees split evenly, but this did not dissuade the state from implementing a suffrage law. Skinner and the jury apparently considered this as critical evidence, as though the grant of suffrage and its support by a segment of the tribe, or by the whole tribe for that matter, was inconsistent with tribal identity. What the court did not understand—and perhaps did not care to—was that the efforts to make Indians citizens and their lands alienable were not unique to Massachusetts. Such efforts had been attempted by New York in the 1840s and again in the 1880s and by Rhode Island with the Narragansetts in 1880 and became national policy with the passage of the General Allotment Act. In all these cases, there were Indians who supported the efforts, but whether allotment occurred or citizenship was granted had little to do with tribal desires.

The plaintiff made a second and more fundamental challenge to the court: that the instructions were so flawed that the jury could not have understood them. While acknowledging that "during the long colloquy with counsel after the instruction, confusion was compounded by my contradictory statements," of the applicable rule, Skinner held that the errors were of no import because they were made out of earshot of the jury. This was only partially true for the judge gave at least one pair of contradictory instructions to the jurors which necessitated his calling them from their deliberations to clarify. One must wonder, if the judge was confused, could the jury be any less so? And if the jurors did not clearly understand the applicable laws and rules upon which they were to base their evaluation of fact, how valid could their findings be? Was it not possible that they found for the defendant for spurious reasons? They had, for example, presented a finding of no tribe in 1790 and the presence of a tribe in 1834 and 1842, clearly inconsistent with the instructions.

It is difficult to read the trial record without getting the impression that the case had less to do with the issue of whether the Mashpees were a tribe than with the social and economic ramifications of a finding for the plaintiff. Skinner made clear this concern in a footnote to the decision. Commenting on the jury's finding that the Mashpees were not a tribe for the purposes of the Indian Trade and Intercourse Acts, he wrote:

> The standards of that Act [Indian Trade and Intercourse Act of 1790], at least as I have interpreted it, require that a tribe demonstrate a definable organization before it can qualify *for the extraordinary remedy of the total voiding of land titles acquired in good faith and without fraud.* Nothing herein, or in answers of the jury, should be taken as holding or implying that the Mashpee Indians are not a tribe for other purposes, including participation in other federal or state programs, concerning which I express no opinion. (Ibid.:950; emphasis added)

It may be that this underlying concern with the remedy, which was not at issue in this trial, led Judge Skinner to rationalize the jury's contradictory findings on tribal existence. Certainly his statement in the footnote limiting the finding to the Indian Trade and Intercourse Acts, magnanimous as it may appear, was in reality both fatuous and condescending because the decision effectively closed to the Mashpees the recognition they needed to benefit fully from federal statutes and protections.

The plaintiff promptly appealed the decision to the United States Court of Appeals, First Circuit, in Boston. The court set oral arguments for November 8, 1978. Besides the question of jury tampering, the plaintiff raised six issues:

1. Should the district court have granted a continuance pending action on a request for federal recognition by the Department of Interior?

2. What is the proper legal definition of a tribe for the purposes of the Indian Trade and Intercourse Acts?

3. If the *Montoya* decision is the basis for the definition of tribe, what is the nature of political author-

ity and to what degree must tribal leaders "order the
lives of members"?

4. Why should the burden of proof on the issue of
tribal status be upon the plaintiff?

5. Were the results of the jury's deliberation "irrec-
oncilably inconsistent and fatally ambiguous" as the
plaintiff alleged?

6. Finally, had the district court sufficiently investigated the effect of the anonymous call on the verdict?

Oral arguments lasted about an hour, and questions from
the three-judge panel were few and superficial. On February 18,
1979, the Court of Appeals rendered its opinion rejecting each
of the plaintiff's contentions and affirming the judgment of the
district court. It rejected a defense request for an advisory opinion on what is referred to as the "white settlement" exception
to the Indian Trade and Intercourse Act of 1834. This ambiguous provision of the act was used to imply assimilation where
Indian communities were surrounded by non-Indian communities. It also refused, by a two-to-one vote, to find that the
district court's definition of a tribe was correct as a matter of
law. The dissenting justice, Bownes, took the position that "both
the district court's delineation of what consitutes 'tribe' as well
as this court's extensive explication should, in my opinion, serve
as a firm foundation for future cases dealing with this sensi-
tive and difficult issue. I would not shy away from reliance on
these instructions and our comments thereon in future cases"
(592 F:2d 1979:595). In light of the United States Supreme
Court's subsequent refusal to review the case, the "shyness" on
the part of the two justices was at least fortuitous.

Ironically, much of the case hinged on the definition of
tribe adopted by the court, and in this the plaintiff carried the
argument but the defense won the decision. In a manner of
speaking, the plaintiff was impaled on legal points of its own
making. Equally ironic, within a year of the trial and while

the appeals were in progress, the Department of the Interior published the procedures for tribal recognition (Federal Register, September 5, 1978 43 [172]:39361–64). A continuance for a year might have removed the need for the trial and allowed a test of the real question in this case: the ownership of the land in Mashpee.

Beyond the issues of law and the appropriateness of the definition of *tribe* applied in this case, there is the equally important issue of the facts of Mashpee history. Are the Mashpees descended from aboriginal people who had inhabited the region at the time of European contact? Had they maintained continuously a separate community that exercised authority over its members? How had they managed to maintain a thirteen-thousand-acre land base, surrounded by rapacious white communities through the eighteenth and most of the nineteenth centuries, how had they ultimately lost that land base, and how had the community adjusted to the changes imposed on it by the Commonwealth of Massachusetts? And finally, are the Mashpees a tribe within the meaning of the Indian Trade and Intercourse Acts? To answer these questions it is necessary to present the history of this Indian people.

❖ 4 ❖

THE GOD OF THE ENGLISH
WAS OFFENDED . . .

T HE ANCESTORS of the present-
day Mashpee Indians of Cape
Cod were an Algonquian-speaking people who shared cultural
traditions with a number of groups in southern New England
under the name of Massachusett-Narragansett (Snow 1978:65).
Bert Salwen (1978:69) refers to these groups as the Pokanoket,
a term synonymous with their more common designation as
Wampanoag. The Indians on Cape Cod shared a common language with the inhabitants of southern Massachusetts and the
northern part of Rhode island, although there were dialect differences among the specific groups. For example, the dialect
spoken on Martha's Vineyard differed enough from that spoken on the Cape and Nantucket as to make communications
difficult (Goddard 1978:72).

The first known recorded description of these people was
provided by Giovanni di Verrazzano, who, in 1524, spent several weeks exploring the area between Block Island and Buz-
zard's Bay. Verrazzano described the people as being handsome,
well dressed, and friendly. He had sailed along most of the east
coast and wrote:

> These people are the most beautiful and have the most
> civil customs that we have found on this voyage. They

are taller than we are; they are a bronze color, some tending more toward whiteness, others to a tawny color; the
face is clear-cut; the hair is long and black, and they take
great pains to decorate it; the eyes are black and alert,
and their manner is sweet and gentle, very like the manner of the ancients. I shall not speak to Your Majesty of
the other parts of the body, since they have all the pro-
portions belonging to any well-built man. Their women
are just as shapely and beautiful; very gracious, of attractive manner and pleasant appearance; their customs and
behavior follow womanly custom as far as befits human
nature; they go nude except for a stag skin embroidered
like the men's, and some wear rich lynx skins on their
arms; their bare heads are decorated with various orna-
ments made of braids of their own hair which hang down
over their breasts on either side. Some have other hair
arrangements such as the women of Egypt and Syria wear,
and these women are older and have been joined in wed-
lock. Both men and women have various trinkets hang-
ing from their ears as the Orientals do; and we saw that
they had many sheets of worked copper which they prize
more than gold. . . . They are very generous and give
away all they have. We made great friends with them,
and one day before we entered the harbor with the ship,
when we were lying at anchor one league out to sea because of unfavorable weather, they came out to the ship
with a great number of their boats; they had painted and
decorated their faces with various colors, showing us that
it was a sign of happiness. (Wroth 1970:138)

Verrazzano and the natives appear to have maintained a
friendly relationship for they made frequent visits to his ship
and permitted him to make excursions into the interior, where
he found "the fields extend for XXV to XXX leagues; they are
open and free of any obstacles or trees, and so fertile that any
kind of seed would produce excellent crops" (ibid.:139). He noted
the abundance of natural resources, the quantities and diver-
sity of fruits, nuts, and game, and the lithic technology that
enabled them to construct "their little boats with a single log

of wood, hollowed out with admirable skill; there is ample room in them for fourteen to XV men" (ibid.).

Most important, Verrazzano observed and reported on aspects of Indian social and political organization. He visited settlements where he found houses, twelve paces or so in circumference, made of split logs and covered with straw, wherein twenty-five to thirty persons lived. The natives, he noted, shifted residences, depending upon the season and the availability of food. Their main staple was a corn gruel to which they added either fresh or dried meats and fish. An implication that the households were organized along patrilineal lines is strengthened by his observation that he met "two kings, who were as beautiful of stature and build as I can possibly describe" (ibid.: 138) and who appeared to exercise control over a retinue of followers.

In 1602, Bartholomew Gosnold sailed along the New England coast and on May 15 arrived in the vicinity of Cape Cod. He noted that game, fish, and berries were plentiful; met and traded with the Indians for tobacco, deer skins, and fish; and observed the abundance of copper ornamentation (Purchas 1905:305-7). On June 5, while busy building a fort and gathering sassafras, Gosnold's crew was visited by a contingent of fifty natives, "stout and lustie men with their Bowes and Arrowes, amongst them there seemed to be one of authoritie, because the rest made an inclining respect unto him" (ibid.: 310). After an anxious moment, gifts were exchanged and the Indians departed; however, on the eleventh, the crew was attacked by a small number of Indians. Shortly thereafter, Gosnold sailed for home with his cargo of sassafras (ibid.:312-13). The following year Martin Pring sailed along the coast of the Cape and observed fields of corn, tobacco, and squash near a village, which he assumed was abandoned (ibid.:326). Pring's objective, like Gosnold's was to collect sassafras, and his crew, too, became involved in skirmishes with the Indian inhabitants.

By far the most complete description of Indian life on the Cape comes from the journal of Samuel de Champlain, who in 1606 paid an extended visit to the area. He sailed along the coast approaching the Cape from the north and followed the sinuous shore, recording the depth of the bays and the features of the land. He visited Indians in their villages, observed their agriculture and technology, and reported on aspects of their political system. His descriptions are succinct but detailed. With respect to subsistence he wrote:

> Before reaching their wigwams, we entered a field planted with Indian corn in the manner I have already described. The corn was in flower and some five and half feet in height. There was some less advanced, which they sow later. We saw an abundance of Brazilian beans, many edible squashes of various sizes, tobacco, and roots which they cultivate, the latter having the taste of an artichoke. The woods are oaks, nut-trees, and full of very fine cypresses [cedars], which are of a reddish colour and have a very pleasant smell. There were also several fields not cultivated, for the reason that the Indians let them lie fallow. When they wish to plant them they set fire to the weeds and then dig up the field with their wooden spades. Their wigwams are round, and covered with heavy thatch made of reeds. In the middle of the roof is an opening, about a foot and a half wide, through which issues the smoke of their fire. We asked them if they had their permanent residence in this place, and whether there was much snow. But we could not find this out very well since we did not understand their language, although they attempted to explain by signs, taking up sand in their hand, then spreading it on the ground, and indicating that the snow was the same colour as our collars, and fell to the depth of a foot. Others indicated that it was less, giving us also to understand that the harbour never froze over; but we were unable to ascertain whether the snow lasted a long time. I consider, however, that this country is temperate and the winter not severe. (Champlain 1922 1:351–52)

Champlain felt less than admiration for the Indians. Though he found them physically attractive, he thought they lacked religion and government and were prone to thievery. Champlain's party had several conflicts with the natives, resulting in the death of at least one sailor. Like his predecessors, Champlain gave the clear impression that the area was well populated with stable and long-term settlements.

These reports and others provide some view of the social, economic, and political systems of the region around the time of contact. According to Dean Snow, the population of southeastern New England in 1600 approached 21,200, with a density of 193 per hundred square kilometers (1980:33). The people lived in villages located some distance from the coast. The villages were moved periodically when the soil and wood supply were depleted. Periodically during the year, the population shifted to fishing stations along the rivers or to the beaches to exploit the abundant shellfish resources. Deer provided the principal source of meat, possibly as much as 90 percent of the total dietary intake (Salwen 1978:160). Small game and waterfowl supplemented the diet. In addition to wild game and seafood, the inhabitants of the region consumed a wide variety of wild plants, but agricultural products provided the main sustenance. Surplus corn, nuts, and dried beans were stored underground in baskets. Thus the distribution and availability of resources in the environment of southern New England and on the Cape resulted in a semipermanent residency pattern, with seasonal movements to exploit a variety of resources.

Although evidence is incomplete, it is likely that villages consisted of ten to twenty wigwams, each of which could hold forty to fifty people. Villages probably consisted of several patrilineal extended families which exhibited a tendency toward patrilocality; however, the matter is far from settled. According to Snow, "Residence with the man's family after marriage may have been a strong principle, but there is evidence that residence was optional or perhaps even tending toward residence with the woman's family in some places in AD 1600" (1980:76).

The political structure centered around the village, which was the basic social unit of these groups. Salwen (1978:166–67) notes:

The village was the basic sociopolitical unit, just as it was
the basic subsistence unit. Day-to-day leadership was provided by the village chief or sachem. Early European ob-
servers often characterize the Indian political system as
"monarchical" (Williams 1936:140), but descriptions of
specific events clearly indicate that sachems had very little coercive power and maintained their influence largely
through persuasion and generosity. Important decisions
were always arrived at in consultation with the "great men"
of the village (Gookin 1972:120), who may have com-
prised a more or less formal sachem's council. (Winslow
1910:345)

There is some evidence that chiefly positions descended
through specific patrilines and could devolve on women as well
as men. Thus the basic political unit of southern New England,
including Cape Cod, at the time of first European settlement,
was the small village consisting of a number of extended families, led by a council of elders and a chief or sachem whose
position was based, at least nominally, on heredity, and whose
power was circumscribed and dependent on the consent of the
members of the village and his or her ability to persuade (Brasser 1971).

Beyond the village level, there existed multi-village alli-
ances, which were loose and tangential organizations with
no centralized authority. It is likely that nothing analogous
to a modern concept of a tribe existed before the seventeenth
century. This development was more the product of contact,
trade, and European settlement and political processes than indigenous development. The problem of dealing with these
pan-village associations has been most effectively resolved by
Salwen. As he points out:

Any attempt to define "tribal" units must face these ethnographic and historical realities. Hence, though many
nineteenth-century local and regional historians and some
twentieth-century ethnologists (Speck 1928a, 1928d, and
Swanton 1952 are the most extreme examples) have at-

tempted to define sharply bounded geographic territories
and to assign long lists of villages and individuals to
each, this account will utilize a less precise, but probably
more realistic, framework, based in part on linguistic evidence and in part on the sometimes conflicting seven-
teenth-century documentation. (Salwen 1978:168)

Using a variety of sources, Salwen organizes the Indian
population into six groups: Pawtucket, Massachusett, Pokanoket, Narragansett, Pequot-Mohegan, and an unnamed residual
group. The Indians on the Cape, along with those on Martha's
Vineyard and Nantucket, are included within the Pokanoket
or Wampanoag. No single leader emerges from the documents
until 1621, when Massasoit and his brother Quadequina negotiated a treaty of friendship with the Plymouth Colony. Massasoit continued to exert influence until his death in 1662, but
it is not clear to what degree that influence extended to the Cape
Cod villages or was based on precontact political structures.
It is certain that he had communications with people on the
Cape. In 1621, he was able to inform Plymouth Colony that
one of its lost members was at Nauset, although he does not
seem to have effected the man's return (Bradford 1908:118–19).

The political and territorial divisions on Cape Cod during the early contact period are equally difficult to ascertain.
In part this may be the result of the cursory nature of European visits, the difficulty of communication, and the general
hostility between the Indians and the Europeans. In 1623, Edward Winslow identified four sachems on the Cape: Cana-
com at Manomet, Iyanough around Yarmouth and eastern
Barnstable, Aspinet at Eastham, and an unnamed one at Ma-
nomoyick in the vicinity of Chatham (1910:304–11). The information is too sketchy to establish the relationship among
these sachems or to those on the mainland. In all likelihood
there were other sachems representing individual villages
throughout the Cape whose names were never recorded. What
little evidence there is indicates that the sachems and their
councils were autonomous at home (ibid.:315). The Dutchman

Isaack deRasieres, who visited the Cape and the Plymouth Colony in 1627, gives one of the best contemporary descriptions of Indian decision making.

> Their political government is democratic, they have a chief Sackima whom they choose by election, who generally is he who is richest in sewan (wampum), through of less consideration in other respects, When any stranger comes, they bring him to the Sackima. On first meeting they do not speak — they smoke a pipe of tobacco; that being done, the Sackima asks: "Whence do you come?" The stranger then states that, and further what he has to say, before all who are present or choose to come. That being done the Sackima announces his opinion to the people, and if they agree thereto, they give all together a sigh — He — and they do not approve, they keep silence, and all come close to the Sackima, and each sets forth his opinion till they agree: that being done, they come all together again to the stranger, to whom the Sackima then announces what they have determined, with the reasons moving them thereto. (Jameson 1959:109)

Whatever the nature of the political structure at the time of contact, European presence, settlement, epidemics, and missionary activity had an immediate and disruptive effect. The first English settlement after Plymouth colony was a trading post at Manomet in 1627, followed by the towns of Sandwich in 1637, Yarmouth in 1639, and eastern Barnstable in 1639–40 (Bradford 1908:22). These and later settlements dislocated the Indians of the area, restricting their access to traditional sites, and increasing the number of disputes between the settlers and the inhabitants.

Even before settlement, the European presence was felt in southern New England and on the Cape. Between 1617 and 1619, an epidemic struck the Wampanoags, killing upward of 90 percent of the population in some places. "I passed alongst the Coast," reported Thomas Dermer in 1619, "where I found some ancient Plantations, not long since populous now utterly void; in other places a remnant remains, but not free of sickness. Their disease the Plague, for we might perceive the sores of such as usually die" (1906:130). The epidemic's effect was uneven only in the amount of loss, not in its distribution. The Cape felt its effects along with the mainland. The epidemic reached its height between 1617 and 1619.

Smallpox continued to kill for the remainder of the century and well into the next. The native population of Martha's Vineyard, for example, was estimated to be around 3,000 in 1642 when the first English settlement was made. This population may already have been affected by disease. By 1720 the population had been reduced to 800, and by 1764 it had fallen to 313 (Jennings 1975:16). The epidemic of the second decade of the seventeenth century had an appalling and immediate effect on Indian communities, but continued outbreaks of disease more quietly and less noticeably destroyed the social and political fabric of native life, disrupting the communities and resulting in a depopulation that facilitated English settlement.

Epidemics took a heavy toll on the Cape well into the 1620s. For example, colonial officials in Plymouth, fearing that the sachems on the Cape were going to join with Indians on the mainland in an attack on the colony, sent an expedition to the Cape to investigate. In 1623, Winslow reported:

> Concerning those other people, that intended to join with the Massacheuseuks against us, though we never went against any of them: yet this sudden and unexpected execution, together with the just judgement of God upon their guilty consciences, hath so terrified and amazed them, as in like manner they forsook their houses, running to and fro like men distracted, living in swamps amongst themselves, whereof very many are dead; as Canacum, the sachem of Manomet, Aspinet, the sachem of Nauset, and Ianough, sachem of Mattachieset. This sachem in his life, in the midst of these distractions, said the God of the English was offended with them, and would destroy them in his anger; and certainly it is strange to hear how many of late have, and still daily die amongst them. Neither

is there any likelihood it will easily cease; because through
fear they set little or no corn, which is the staff of life,
and without which they cannot long preserve health and
strength. (1910:344)

Three facts in the above passage stand out. First, a major
segment of Indian leadership on the Cape was destroyed in
1623. Second, the Indians were suffering from more than the
effects of a single epidemic; serious economic dislocation resulting in famine added to the debilitating effects of disease.
Third, attendant with the mortality was severe disruption in
the social and political fabric. The epidemic struck sachem,
powwow, and commoner, male and female, young and old,
with swift impartiality so that in a short time the principal
bearers of the ritual and political life were gone.

After the 1620s the Cape Indians were incapable of successfully waging war against Plymouth Colony. The settlements
that were made in the 1630s came on what Jennings has ap-
propriately called "widowed land" (1975). It is no coincidence
that the settlements at Manomet in the 1620s and those at Sandwich, Yarmouth, and Barnstable in the following decade occurred in areas that had been depopulated by disease.

English settlement continued well into the 1640s, when
the public record shows the first mention of the Indians at
Mashpee. In 1648, Paupmunnuck, "with the consent of his
brother, and all the rest of his associates," sold a piece of land
to Barnstable (PCR 2:125). This sale, coupled with previous
ones, physically separated the Indians at Mashpee from those
to the east. This transaction led to a boundary dispute in 1658,
which was settled by establishing the boundary line along the
Santuit River and around Santuit Pond, its present location
(ibid.:143–44).

With settlement came the missionaries, who made their
influence felt early in the postcontact period. The charter of
Massachusetts set as its principal objective to "wynn and in-
cite the Natives of [the] country, to the Knowledge and Obedience of the onlie true God and Savior of Mankinde, and the

Christian Fayth" (Records of Massachusetts 1:17, as quoted in Jennings 1975:230). The inability of native healers to treat the sick and remove the scourge led to dismay in the villages and further deprivation among the survivors. In theocratic Plymouth, churches were among the first structures to be erected and ministers were quick to seek the conversion of the natives, a process made easier by their losses and dislocation but more difficult by the scattered abodes of the remaining groups. The solution was to bring these disparate remnants to a few locations and establish Christian Indian towns, where their spiritual needs, if not their worldly ones, could be met. Mashpee suited this purpose admirably. It had a resident Indian population that remained largely intact through the early years of English settlement. The settlement process resulted in the Indian community being surrounded on three sides by English settlements, thus isolating it from other Indians. English settlers did not covet the land; they recognized native land tenure, which was secured by colonial charter. Finally, there was available a missionary, Richard Bourne, with sufficient zeal to serve the South Sea Indians, as these Indians at Mashpee were sometimes called.

Bourne first appears in the historical records of the 1650s as a selectman for the town of Sandwich. In 1655, the General Court "granted unto Richard Bourne, of Sandwidge, to make use of som upland meddow lying att the end of Mashpee Pond, provided hee doe it with the concent of the Indians to whom it belongeth" (PCR 3:65). Bourne's influence among the Indians in Mashpee grew during the decade. He was involved in the boundary settlement in 1658 and, shortly thereafter, established himself as missionary to the Mashpees.

There is no doubt that the South Sea Indians had a long and continuous occupancy in the area. Axtell points out that later seventeenth- and eighteenth-century documents refer to the Mashpees' occupancy from "time out of mind, essentially" (TT 5:40, 41). Geography contributed to their insularity. Access to the Mashpee area was blocked to the north by a ridge while to the south the shoreline provided no good harbor for ships. In addition, the waters off the Mashpee shore are relatively shallow, making navigation hazardous. Finally, the Cape is widest at this point, inhibiting communications and transportation. Thus a combination of factors led to Mashpee's relative isolation with the result that the precontact political structures persisted somewhat intact until the expanding English population brought the South Sea Indians into contact, contract, and litigation with their white neighbors.

It is impossible to describe in any detail the physical organization of the Indian community in Mashpee, but it is certain that there were recognized political leaders. In 1648, Paupmunnuck sold land to Barnstable in behalf of the tribe. In 1662, a dispute occurred between the Mashpees and one John Allen "concerning a mare killed by the Indians att Mashpee" (PCR 4:17). Paupmunnuck and Keencomsett agreed to pay Allen the sum of fourteen pounds in commodities as indemnity.

These men appear to be the earliest named leaders in the Indian community, but they were by no means the only leaders in the area. With the assistance of preacher Richard Bourne, the sachems Wepquish and Tookenchosin, in 1665, gave over to the South Sea Indians the land in and around Mashpee, Santuit, and Cotuit "forever, soe as never to be given, sold, or alienated from them without all theire consents" (PCR 6:159). The following year Bourne and his son Sheirjashub witnessed a grant by Quatchatisset, sachem of Manomet, to the South Sea Indians for the same land (MA 33:149–50).

Bourne was active in other areas besides preaching and the witnessing of deeds. He was able to get the Mashpees to shift their political system to the type commonly found in other praying towns. He petitioned the General Court to approve a council of six consisting of Paupmunnuck, Keencomsett, Watanamatucke, Nanquidnumacke, Kanoonus, and Mocrust, "to have the chiefe inspection and management thereof, with the healp and advise of the said Richard Bourne, as the matter may require; and that one of the aforesaid Indians bee by the rest instaled to acte as a constable amongst them, it being alwaies provided, notwithstanding, that what homage acostomed

Mashpee Indian Powwow, ca. 1929. Photograph courtesy of Russell Peters.

Powwow Sunday at the Old Indian Church, Mashpee, 1936. Photograph courtesy of Russell Peters.

North Mashpee School

The North Mashpee School. Built around 1891, it was replaced by a brick structure in 1940 that has since become the Mashpee Town Hall. Drawing by Pedro Lopez Santiago, courtesy of Russell Peters.

The Mashpee Town Hall as it looked at the beginning of the twentieth century. Drawing by Pedro Lopez Santiago, courtesy of Russell Peters.

The Hotel Attaquin, built around 1840 by Solomon Attaquin, was a favorite vacation site for non-Indians, including Henry Thoreau, Daniel Webster, and James Farley. It was destroyed by fire in 1954. Drawing by Pedro Lopez Santiago, courtesy of Russell Peters.

Russell Peters, president of the Mashpee Wampanoag Tribal Council, making a point at a town meeting. To his left is Joan Tavares; to his right is George Benway. Photograph courtesy of Joyce Dopkeen.

Eben Queppish. Photograph by Frank G. Speck, 1920. Photograph courtesy of Smithsonian Institution, National Museum of the American Indian.

Facing page: Vernon Pocknet, president of the Mashpee Wampanoag Tribal Council, speaking at a public meeting. Photograph courtesy of Joyce Dopkeen.

legally due to any superior sachem bee not hereby infringed" (PCR 4:80). In 1670 Bourne organized the Indian church and led the Mashpees into the fold (Gookin 1970:57).

The decade of the 1660s was a period of transition and coalescence for the Mashpee community. Its geographical limits were defined and guaranteed, with title vested in the group. The political system shifted to one that more closely reflected the English ideal of Indian government, with political allegiance to the Crown and colony replacing the more nebulous ties to other sachems. The council of six differed little in its functions from its aboriginal antecedent. Its acceptance by the General Court of the colony certainly enhanced its power, although the previous structure appears to have had sufficient power to commit the group, as witness the sale of land and the agreement to pay indemnity. Kinship continued to be the basis for determining group membership and took on new importance because it was synonymous with membership in the landholding group. In all likelihood, residency and subsistence patterns remained unchanged. Although few population statistics are available for this period, it is reasonable to suggest that the tribe was small, perhaps no more than two hundred or so. In 1674 Bourne reported ninety-five "praying Indians" at Mashpee (ibid.: 56–57).

The South Sea Indians retained considerable autonomy over their internal affairs, but they were subject to the influence and counsel of the colony through their missionary, Richard Bourne. They were subject, too, to the laws of the General Court, to which they had pledged their allegiance. The General Court became the arbiter in disputes between the colonists and the Mashpees. In time a tension developed between the colonists and the Mashpees as the former pressed to gain control of all aspects of Indian political and social life. The tribe vigorously resisted. These multiple pressures helped form the Mashpee Indians out of the indigenous population and created for their sole use a reservation of land.

In 1675–76, the colony of Massachusetts engaged in its second war against the native populations, this time with the

Narragansetts and Wampanoags. The Mashpees, along with other groups on the Cape, had pledged their allegiance to the English and thus remained neutral when the colonists slaughtered King Philip and his allies (PCR 5:70–71). Neutrality was providential. The war destroyed what military power remained on the mainland but brought no changes in the political situation of the praying towns on the Cape. In 1685, the Mashpee Indians petitioned the General Court to recognize the lands ceded them by Quebquish and Tookenchosin and by Quatchatisset twenty years before (PCR 6:159–60). The court agreed to "confirme said land to the said Indians, to be perpetually to them and their children, as that no part of them shall be granted to or purchased by any English whatsoever, by the Court's allowance, without the consent of all the said Indians" (ibid.:160).

The English colonies were no more immune to political upheaval than were their native counterparts. The seventeenth century saw the rise and demise of Cromwell, the reestablishment of the Stuart monarchy, and the Glorious Revolution. Distance provided no protection against these upheavals, and colonial governments were removed and political structures altered. Changes in the colonies in turn affected the Indian communities. In 1691, the Crown issued a royal charter incorporating Plymouth and Maine into Massachusetts, thereby abolishing the separate government of Plymouth. In 1693–94 Massachusetts acted to increase its control over the Indian towns "to the intent that the Indians may be forwarded in civility and Christianity, and that drunkenness and other vices be more effectually suppressed amongst them" (ARMB 1693–94 2d sess., chap. 17:150–51). The law provided for the appointment of agents to review the actions of Indian governments and empowered the agents to punish criminal offenses according to the laws of the province. There is no evidence that the agents played any active role in Mashpee affairs.

Bourne's long tenure as minister for the Mashpees ended in 1685, and he was succeeded by Simon Popmonit, the first of a long series of Indian ministers and tribal leaders. In 1698, a delegation from the Society for the Propagation of the Gospel visited Mashpee and reported, "They are in general well clothed, being in number 57 families, in which are from ten years old and upwards 263 persons, divers of whom have the character of very sober men. The Indian preacher here is Simon Papmonit [sic], a person suitably qualified as most among them for that work. Their rulers are Caleb Papmonit, Caleb Pohgneit, Sancohsin, James Ketah. Here they want a schoolmaster" (MHS Collections, ser. 1, 10:133).

The discrepancy between Bourne's figure of 94 praying Indians in 1674 and the above count may indicate that Bourne counted only adults or the population may have increased because of new arrivals in the community. It is also possible that the 1698 count was inflated to justify more aid from missionary societies. Certainly some increase in population could be expected because the Mashpees were not involved in war and there is no evidence of widespread disease at this time. The document reflects another change: the leaders installed by the General Court at Plymouth were gone, replaced by a smaller group. Instead of six, only four leaders were mentioned, and only the name Popmonit appeared on both lists. There is no indication of how political power was transferred, but the probability is that it moved within influential families, particularly ones tied to the religious structure. Names like Popmonit, Pohgneit, and Ketah appear consistently throughout the next two hundred years.

The first decades of the eighteenth century were marked by increasing conflict between the colonists and the Mashpees. Encroachments by settlers from Barnstable led the Mashpees to petition for redress in 1710 (MA 31:68–69), with the result that Massachusetts appointed a commission to investigate (ARMB 1779–80, chap. 6:778–79, Town Chapters 1710). Again, in 1717, residents from Barnstable complained of boundary problems, stating, "That they are unwilling to contend with the said Indians in the Common Law by Reason of the Poverty of the said Indians and other Inconveniences, And therefore pray this court to take some suitable and effective Method of Ascertaining and Setting the Boundaries of the said Land to prevent any future Disputes" (ARMB 1717–18, chap. 151:577).

A commission was appointed, which, in March 1717, met with both parties and worked out a boundary settlement (ibid. 1718–19, chap. 18:595). Similar disputes arose in 1735 (ibid. 1735–36, chap. 123:177) and in 1741 (ibid. 1741–43, chap. 32: 26). These instances are of interest not because land disputes occurred but for the vigor with which the Mashpees prosecuted their claims and defended their rights. Left largely to their own devices, the Mashpees developed mechanisms to manage their internal affairs as well as spokesmen to deal with the colonial government. Their political system paralleled that of the New England town meeting, but it was not a replica. As they stated in one of their many petitions: "We had meeting and chose officers among ourselves and appointed men to oversee our lands and marsh and take care that everyone had his share and no more" (MA 32:415–16). The petition goes on to report the troubles the Indians had with their neighbors because of the rules and orders they had instituted. It suggests that another change in the organization of the Mashpee government had taken place, for the purpose of the meeting had been to select overseers. Axtell (TT 5:79), in a discussion of this shift, argues that the proprietary system was introduced by the Mashpees some time around 1723. The proprietors had to be members of the Mashpee community and of Indian descent. The tribe owned the land that was allotted to proprietors for their use. Children could inherit allotments and improvements, but if a proprietor died without heirs, the land reverted to the tribe. Tribal membership assured the individual the right to land, and, conversely, having a right to land identified an individual as a member of the group. Descent from a proprietor thus became a defining characteristic of tribal membership. The system of land tenure adopted by the Mashpees at the behest of their missionary represented no major departure from custom. Aboriginal land practice provided for the allotment of parcels of land for agricultural use by members of the extended family. The deeds of the 1660s prevented the disposal of land to colonists, thus assuring the families that resided in Mashpee the use of the land and the tribe the title. It did not disturb or alter the existing land practice. The same holds true for the adoption of a proprietary; it was a change that made sense to the English and little difference to the Mashpees.

Massachusetts instituted a change in 1746 that did make a difference. A law was passed providing for the appointment of three guardians for each Indian settlement. These guardians had the power "to take into their hands the said Indians' lands, and allot to the several Indians of the several plantations such parts of the said lands and meadows as shall be sufficient for their particular improvement" (ARMB 1746–47, chap. 12:306–7). Surplus lands could be leased to settlers, and the money would be used for the support of tribal members at the discretion of the guardians. The Mashpees, through their leaders, vehemently opposed this act and protested to the General Court of Massachusetts:

> We poor Indians Entreat the great Court at Boston to remove those gentlemen the Honble Coll. Bourn Jeams Otis Eq., and Mr. Crocker From being our Guardians, for we are more hirt since they have intermeddled about our lands and medows, for we are now destitute, and likely to starve to death with hunger or for want, for they stop our money, and we lived better before they come, and when they first come we was still and hoped we should then do better, but now we see we are poorer. We do humbly beseech our Honourable Rulers to take care of us that they may not have power to sell our land to any for we never desire that it should be sold but that we and our children may live upon it if god be willing. We have never been against the English but united with them against their enemies, therefore we hope you will help. (MA 31:102)

The petition went on to describe in detail the privation resulting from the legislative action.

The General Court turned a deaf ear to the petition, but this did not stop the protest. Undaunted, the Mashpees petitioned again in December 1753, claiming that they were facing ruin, that the guardians lived too far away from them to spend sufficient time on Mashpee affairs, and that when the guardians did meet they did so at a tavern: "There we go and some of us gitt too much liquor and lately there was fighting and quarreling there, and some of us abused by English men and we know not what to do" (ibid. 32:424–26a).

The General Court's appointment of overseers did not represent a negation of tribal authority. The act placed no restraints on the tribe's control over its internal affairs except over the allocation of land, and the Mashpees retained final control over its alienation. For example, the law denying the Mashpee petition of complaint of 1747 contained a provision allotting some land to the Mashpee minister Solomon Briant "for his own improvement or allow him the Incomes of such share, Provided that a Major Part of the Proprietors regularly assembled shall pass a Vote for that purpose" (ARMB 1747–52, chap. 130). The law attempted one modification of the rules regarding alienation established by the original land deed and long usage, and that was to substitute a majority vote for a unanimous one. It is unclear whether the Mashpees acknowledged this change. Again, in 1758–59, when the Mashpees desired to convey five acres to their new minister, Gideon Hawley, the legislature ordered the guardians to notify the Mashpees that they were free to choose three persons to execute a conveyance (MA 33:67–67a).

Unable to get the General Court to remove the overseers, the Mashpees took their appeal to the king. They sent Reuben Cognehew, "a Mohegan [Mashpee] Indian of the Tribes community known by the name of the South Sea Indians in behalf of himself and the rest of the said Tribe of Indians" (ibid.:146–48) to lay their complaint before the Crown. In his petition Cognehew recounted the history of the Mashpee Indian land claim, the frequent encroachments by English settlers, and the failure of the Massachusetts Bay Colony to protect the rights of the three hundred Mashpees. Cognehew then recounted the travails of his journey to England, which amounted to a minor odyssey.

That your petitioner accordingly embarked himself on board a vessel ready to sail from Rhode Island, the master of which pretended he was bound to England, but instead thereof falsely and inhumanly carried your Petitioner to the West Indies, but Almighty was pleased to frustrate his wicked designs by causing the vessel to be shipwrecked on the coast of Hispaniola.

That your Petitioner with the rest of the crew with difficulty got on shoar, and were soon after taken off by one of your Majestys Ships of War, the captain of which impressed your Petitioner and the rest of the crew to serve on board your Majestys Fleet at Jamaica, where your Petitioner having made his case known to Admiral Coates obtained his discharge and soon after took his passage to England in a merchant ship. (Ibid.:146–47)

The Crown ordered an investigation of the matter and, after three years of reports and complaints (ibid.:151, 152, 156, 177–85), colonial policy was changed. In 1763, Massachusetts incorporated Mashpee as a self-governing district. The government consisted of "five overseers (two of said overseers being Englishmen), a town clerk and treasurer, both English, two wardens and one or more constables." The overseers were empowered to conduct the affairs of the district, including the allotment of land, the regulation of fishing, and the lease of rights to common lands. Further, they were empowered to apply any income to the relief of the indigent, to issue writs of ejectment and trespass, and to call district meetings "as the selectmen of any town in this province by law now have." Finally, the law allowed them "to admit other Indians or mulattoes to be inhabitants and proprietors of said Mashpee" (ARMB 1763, chap. 3:640). To all intents and purposes the law organized the Mashpee tribe as a town; however, it did not impose the same limitations over internal affairs common to New England towns. Whites were to be elected as overseers, yet the Mashpees retained majority control. As a practical matter, political life in Mashpee changed little from the preguardian period.

In many ways, the Mashpee community of the late eighteenth century resembled its aboriginal antecedent. In 1762, Ezra Stiles, president of Yale College, made one of his many sojourns through New England, spending some time on the Cape. He visited Mashpee, along with several other Indian communities, and filled his journal with details of tribal life. He placed the Mashpee population at 250, consisting of about 75 families (Stiles 1916:59). These families, he found, were scattered throughout the plantation living in "about 60 wigwams and 6 houses" (ibid.:167). His map (ibid.:163) shows that there was no village or other definable concentration of population though densities were higher in three areas: Ashumuit Pond, Santuit Pond, and South Cape. This pattern of isolated residences compares favorably with the descriptions given by early explorers, most notably Champlain (1607), and fits the pattern described by Snow (1980). Indian subsistence patterns remained the same throughout the eighteenth century as did native land tenure practices. The dwellings shown on the map closely approximate the location of the so-called "ancient ways," the early pathways used by the Mashpees and still discernible through the maze of contemporary housing developments. Finally, the map supports the view that the Mashpees were geographically, as well as socially, isolated from the white settlers. The bulk of the residences, as well as the church, the principal meeting place, were on the south side of the plantation.

Stiles was struck by an Indian practice of piling up sticks and stones at places along the path. As he described it:

Mr. Williams told me that on the Road from Sandwich to Plymouth there is a large Stone or Rock in a place free of Stones; and that the Indians immemorially have been used, whenever and as often as they pass this large Stone, to cast a Stone or piece of Wood upon it. That Stones not being plenty, pieces of Wood is most commonly used, and that there will once in a few years be a large Pile on the Stone, which is often consumed by the firing of the Woods for Deer. That the Indians continue the Custom to this day, tho' they are a little ashamed the English should see them, and accordingly when walking with an English they have made a path round at a quarter Mile's Distance to avoid it. There is also at a little Distance another Stone which they also inject upon, but pass it with less scruple; but are so scrupulous that none was even known to omit castigating Stones or Wood on the other. . . . The Indians being asked the reason of their Custom and Practice, say they know nothing about it, only that their Fathers and Grandfathers and Great Grandfathers did so, and charged all their children to do so; and yet if they did not cast a Stone or piece of Wood on that Stone as often as they passed by it, they would not prosper, and particularly should not be lucky in hunting Deer. But if English call them the Sacrificing Rocks, tho' the Indians don't imagine it a sacrifice; at least they kill and offer no Animals there, and nothing but Wood and Stones. (Stiles 1916:160)

In the 1920s, Frank Speck photographed and identified the location of two of these piles, which he called "sacrifice heaps" or "taverns." One was at the juncture of Mashpee and Waquoit roads, on an old trail to the shellfish grounds at Waquoit, and the other was at the intersection of a trail that ran from Mashpee village to the Old Indian Church and the road from Santuit (Speck 1928a:126, 128). Apparently, the practice persisted into the twentieth century.

Along with land, residency, and subsistence practices, there was a continuity in political behavior which is obscured by the continual turmoil and vacillations in colonial policies. Caleb Popmonit's political activities spanned more than fifty years; his name first appears in the 1698 report, then on the 1736 petition, and again on the petition of 1750. John Wepquish's name appears in 1736, 1750, and 1753. The same holds true for other individuals, indicating a relatively stable leadership in the community. This leadership seemed to have had a broad-based support, as witnessed by the number of signers to the petitions of 1750 and 1753.

The victory in 1763, which reestablished Mashpee internal autonomy, was short-lived. During the revolutionary war, many of the Mashpee men joined the colonial forces and were lost in action or died of other causes while in service. Axtell (TT 6:30) reports that twenty-five out of twenty-six from one Barnstable regiment died. He estimates the total loss at upward of fifty males, or one-half of the total adult male population (ibid.). Such losses had a calamitous effect on the community. To add to the tribe's problems, the Commonwealth of Massachusetts paid little attention to Indian affairs, preoccupied as it was with national and state concerns. The resulting difficulties prompted four local residents to petition the legislature on behalf of the Mashpees, seeking relief and protection. The petitioners made the following points:

1. The Mashpees had fought on the side of the colonies and had lost most of their men.

2. There were now about eighty families left, many of them headed by widows or women married to "foreign-Negros and Molatoes," who had no right to vote in district meetings.

3. At the last annual meeting there were no more than nineteen eligible voters, "being so small a number they become very easy prey to their white leaders by plying them with spiritous liquor whenever they want any favour they soon obtain them."

4. The overseers had taken control, suppressed opposition, forbade the district clerk to keep a record of proceedings, and conducted the election of the overseers only after they had gotten the electors drunk.

5. The overseers had sent the young men "into the whaling business and their wives and children and the poor indigent families are about among the white people a beging for the necessaries of life in the adjacent Town, their complaints are many grievous." (MA Acts of 1788, May sess., chap. 2)

The petitioners offered no remedy, but the implication was clear: Mashpee needed more regulation. In May 1788, the state passed legislation providing for the appointment of three guardians to manage the affairs of the plantation, thus repealing the act of 1763. The Reverend Gideon Hawley was among the three guardians appointed (ARM 1788, chap. 2:6–9).

The following year, the act was changed to provide for five overseers, who could appoint one or more guardians (ibid. 1788–89, chap. 52:503–4). Although the various memorialists had identified the inability of the Mashpees to govern themselves as the primary reason for the state's assumption of greater control, in reality, the principal cause of the problems at Mashpee was the inability or unwillingness of the state to enforce its laws against non-Indians who trespassed on Mashpee land and swindled the Indians out of their property. "Indian Chiefs," Hawley wrote in 1792, "who act as Overseers and have the property of this district in their power have for several years past, and they are now giving away for Rum their lands, and settling Negroes and others who have emigrated and some from the interior parts of the country, who by means of their connection with the people of my charge are ruining their best interests" (MHS, Hawley Manuscripts).

There was more at work than the customary greed threatening the Indians' title and inspiring white intervention in tribal affairs. An unrelated struggle for political power in a neighboring town led to the combatants using the tribe as a cat's paw. Gideon Hawley provides the following description of the intrigue:

> The winter of 1788 John Painville, as I understood afterwards, was very busy with some of my Indians, and obtained such an interest that he came within one of being chosen at the March-meeting our principal officer. By Dr. Smith's and my influence Deacon Nye had been kept in office for a long course of years. But some grew very weary of his administration. The Fishes and other Whites were against Nye and a very considerable number of Blacks

were uneasy with him. Painville after he lost his election
here, became more restless. Sued Nye (as Squibs attorney)
and obtained against him 50 dollars. As many wished to
get Nye out from his offices in his *own* town and to get
Mr. Bourne into the office of Representative, many things
were said and acted against Nye with great virulency; and
he was represented as being fraudulent to the Indians. I
did not choose to have much to say in these matters, but
had it in view if possible to make some alteration in the
regulation of my people. I did not associate with Painville; but he hove himself in my way. He fished for my
sentiments. I did not suspect him. (Ibid.)

If anything, the failure to govern lay with Massachusetts
and not the Mashpees. The protection of the tribe's resources
was a concern and responsibility assumed by the state, but the
legislation to accomplish this lofty aim was designed with other
base political purposes in mind.

The problem of outsiders settling in Mashpee was particularly vexing. At first glance, it would appear that the Mashpee community consisted predominantly of non-Mashpees,
but a closer study of the documents does not support this conclusion. Hawley sets the population in 1788 at 400 "Black Inhabitants upon these lands," who, he says, "are greatly and
variously mixed as we have only twenty and five males and
about one hundred and ten females, who are truly aboriginal,
and not mixed" (MHS, S. P. Savage Manuscripts). This number does not include minors. Hawley's estimate is a bit high;
an actual enumeration in 1807 gave the population as 357, including children (TT 5:6). Regardless of the precise number,
it is clear that Hawley described the entire tribal population
as black, over half of which he reported were "truly original
and not mixed." In attempting to understand Hawley's use of
the term *black*, Axtell makes the point that English ethnocen-
trism of the seventeenth century applied cultural pejoratives to
denote the status of natives — savages and barbarians — whereas
by the middle of the eighteenth century the phrases in use were

racial and all nonwhites were equated with the lowest status group in the society, which in this case was the blacks. Hawley distinguished nonmembers by referring to them as Negroes. Hawley reported, "The Negro men (who are adults) are as follows, Ceesar Cobb, Ceesar Gorham, George Quanker, Priomy, Prince, Sirio, Ada, Richard Gold, Coffee, and perhaps some others I do not recollect, but not one of these have married female proprietors or by any means acquired a legal right to the soil" (MHS, S. P. Savage Manuscripts: Letter to S. Bourne).

According to Hawley, only two Negroes had married into the tribe and established a legal claim through their wives. In addition, six whites, including four Hessian soldiers, had married in. The revolutionary war had resulted in a serious depopulation of adult males, and there had been no corresponding increase in non-Mashpees to fill the empty hearths. Widows' weeds became the common garment in Mashpee for another generation.

To be sure, the Mashpees had problems with squatters and interference in their internal tribal affairs. One would be hard put to find a tribe east of the Mississippi River that was not not having similar troubles. It was the self-stated responsibility of the state of Massachusetts to protect the land rights of the tribe, a responsibility the state had failed to carry out, as the number and frequency of petitions attest. Mashpee had resources that drew speculators. There were available land, streams, lakes, and bays rich in aquatic life, oak and pine forests, and cheap labor, particularly children. Whites and Negroes moved in and squatted on the land, refusing to pay rent (ARM 1792, chap. 148). The bulk of Mashpee land was covered with forest. Hawley estimated that there were around eight thousand acres of pitch pine and two thousand acres of oak, with another two thousand acres cleared for farming (MHS, Savage Manuscripts). Much of the land in the neighboring towns had been denuded, making this resource particularly valuable. Another resource, labor, was coveted with equal zeal. Children were indentured to whites and "the young Indians their Overseers sent into the Whaling business" (ARM 1788, chap. 2).

Hawley summed up the problem in one of his many appeals to the legislature.

> I have already observed that speculators and Indian trad-
> ers are similar in every part of the country. It is oppor-
> tunity which makes men knaves. There is, perhaps, as
> much honesty among our Cape Cod people, as among
> any other. The Indians have certainly done as well here,
> as anywhere in the United States. Their lands, at Cape
> Cod and Martha's Vineyard, are yet preserved in a good
> degree. But they are more coveted by the white people
> than formerly. Land increases rapidly in value. The peo-
> ple multiply by means of the fisheries. Wood in many of
> the lower towns on the Cape is scarce. At Mashpee it is
> plenty. [   ] numbers have located themselves near this
> plantation and are eagerly anticipating opportunities to
> come into possession of this Indian interest. (ARM, 1795,
> chap. 20)

In some ways, Mashpee at the close of the century mir-
rored the political turmoil and divisions of the surrounding
communities. "These Indians are in parties," Hawley wrote.
"We have Wigs and Tories. . . . We have white and black here
in all their degrees. We have different interests and combina-
tions. . . . They cannot fix upon one in whom they will unite.
Two or three are prevalent here alternatively. They are strug-
gling all around us for power and property." The laws passed
by the legislature did little to alleviate the problems or curtail
the external pressures. Hawley's problems and those of the community were worsened with the arrival of an Indian Baptist
minister in the summer of 1795. Hawley grudgingly admitted
that the new minister was popular "and has got away from my
church three or four whom he has plunged" (MHS, Hawley
Manuscripts, Fact Sheet, Sept. 2, 1795).
    The nearly incessant complaining from Hawley brought
results, although not necessarily the ones he had sought. The
legislature sent a committee to investigate in the summer of
1795. It found that the Indians were dissatisfied with the gov-

ernment structure imposed in 1788 and wanted a return to self-elected officials. The Mashpees complained that under the new law their lands were poorly managed and their monies misused; if the law was a good one, it suffered grievously from poor execution by Hawley, "who from his age and other causes, could not discharge the duties assigned to him." The committee acknowledged the complaints to be factually true but did not recommend any change in the law. It did recommend more frequent meetings of the overseers and more candor on their part in explaining their actions to the Mashpee proprietors, and it urged that new laws be passed to protect the plantation's forest (MA 1808, Report of the Committee of 1795). As a result, the legislature passed a law providing for the removal of unauthorized persons from Mashpee (ARM 1796, chap. 23:52).

At the turn of the century the Mashpees continued to possess their land and retain their identity as a tribe. The political and religious machinations of the inhabitants of the neighboring towns resulted in impingements on their freedom to control their internal affairs, but the reasons for this intervention had little to do with problems within the Indian community, which continued to be a viable social and political unit. Much of the controversy centered around Hawley, who saw self-government in Mashpee as a threat to his religious teachings. In 1802, he wrote, "You may raise a religious fervor for a time among savages, but without law and civil government you cannot establish the Gospel anywhere. . . . Liberty and equality, as it has been presented in our day has not been attended with salutary effects. The minds of common people have been rather injured by that means" (MHS Hawley Manuscripts, 1802). Hawley saw the need for a shepherd to guide the affairs of a pliant flock, protected from the call of other, less worthy servants of God. He did not reckon upon his own frailty, the ambition of others, or the obduracy of the Mashpees. As a result, religious as well as political divisions occurred within the Indian community.

Hawley and others projected on Mashpee their view of the social order, a progression from savagery to civilization.

In the process they added another component, racism. As Axtell has noted, the reference to the Mashpees as blacks was

> the beginning of a racial designation for a people who in the seventeenth century would have been given a strictly religious or cultural designation. In the seventeenth century they would have been referred to as pagans, savages, barbarians, or just plain Indians or natives. By 1740 and 1750, there is enough experience with black slavery in New England that the English are picking up the habit of equating all people of color with the lowest of their scale — the lowest form of color that they know — which is black; and, essentially, regarding an Indian in the same eyes as they would a slave. (TT 6:36)

By this logic, Indians were incapable of self-government; they were children to be raised to a civilized state and isolated from contact with whites until the process had been completed. Indeed, some suggested that the effort was worthless, as witness the following description recorded in 1802:

> It appears from the account which has been given of the plantation, that it has been an expensive establishment from the beginning, but probably little good has been produced. The Indians have become neither a religious nor a virtuous people, nor have they been made happy. No one can doubt the pious and benevolent intentions of Richard Bourne, who procured this expensive patent for the Indians; nor of the gentlemen, who in succession, for a century and a half, have watched over them, like parents over their children. The exertions, which have been made for their benefit, are honorable to the government of Massachusetts, and to the societies who have so liberally contributed their time and wealth; but the melancholy reflection, that they have laboured in vain, perpetually intrudes itself on the mind. With a hundreth part of the pains which have been bestowed on these savages, a town might have been raised up on the ground occupied by them, which would contain four times as many white in-

habitants, enjoying all the comforts of civilized life, and
contributing by their industry to the welfare of the state,
and by their taxes, which they pay, to the support of government. This plantation may be compared to a pasture,
which is capable of feeding fifteen or eighteen hundred
sheep; but into which several good-natured and vision-
ary gentlemen have put three or four hundred wolves,
foxes, and skunks, by way of experiment, with the hope
that they might be in time be tamed. A shepherd has been
placed over them at high wages; and as the animals have
been found to decrease, other wolves, foxes, and skunks
have been allured to the pasture, to keep up their number. But the attempt has been in vain; the wild animals
have worried the shepherd; have howled, and helped, and
cast other indignities upon the gentlemen, who from time
to time have visited them, for the sake of observing how
the experiment went on; and have almost died with hun-
ger, though they have been fed at an enormous expense.
(Freeman 1815:11–12)

After recounting this sad exposition, the writer recommended the maintenance of the plantation. "Let them remain;
and let the pious and benevolent still persevere in their endeav-
ors, however hopeless, to make them good men and christians.
Perhaps when they cease to be Indians, when their blood is
more plentifully mixed with the blood of Africa, they may ac-
quire the habits of temperance and industry; and may become
useful to the state" (ibid.:12). With such colossal cultural my-
opia and self-righteous racism, it is little wonder that the political life of the Mashpees was in nearly constant turmoil.

In 1807, a group of some fifty-seven Mashpees led by Zaccheus Pognit petitioned the state to reduce the number of overseers and allow the proprietors to have a voice in their choice.
In the same year, another group led by Nautumpum petitioned
the legislature not to change the form of government of the
plantation and challenged the assertions in the first petition
(ARM Resolves of 1807, chap. 109). This petition had seventy-
five signers. The argument over governance soon involved

whites from the neighboring community. Also in 1807, John Fish, a resident of Sandwich, gave a deposition in support of the first petition, as did one Lemuel Ewer. Zaccheus Pognit, the leader of the opposition, was subjected to pressure by the supporters of the existing tribal government to recant and sign a petition (Fish). The matter finally came before a joint committee of the legislature, which found in favor of Pognit. The legislature enacted the changes in March 1808, reducing the number of overseers to three (ibid., Act of 1808, chap. 108: 240–41). Once again, the Mashpees had effected a change in their government through petition and protest. Within a decade, the Mashpees sought further changes in government, although this time the legislature did not fully accommodate them (ibid., Resolves of 1818, chap. 89:486–87). The only changes enacted defined membership in the tribe as limited to those who could trace descent from a proprietor and increased the powers of the overseers to control alcohol use and punish violators. In addition, the overseers were vested with the power of guardians (ibid., Act of 1819, chap. 105:161–64).

The end of the second decade of the nineteenth century saw few changes in Mashpee besides those in the political sphere. The tribe's population in 1820 was set at approximately 320; some were farmers and others worked in the whaling and fishing industries. Two denominations, Congregationalist and Baptist, vied for members, and there were the usual allegations of alcohol abuse and immorality alluded to by local missionaries. In less than two hundred years, the Mashpees had faced and adjusted to a long series of convulsive events.

During this period their political system had taken on a more structured appearance and their religious system had been radically altered by Christian doctrine and missionary zeal. Yet, as important as these changes were, they should not obscure the underlying tribal continuity. Throughout the period, they chose their own leaders by consensus, and they managed their own internal affairs, particularly when that management involved the use of land. Occasionally, they admitted individuals to the community, very often spouses of members, but they did not extend full rights to them. In some cases, they were adopted; in others, they were permitted to use the land on which they lived but denied a voice in policy matters. Although within the colony and later state of Massachusetts, they maintained separate social and political boundaries and exhibited a remarkable degree of internal autonomy. Nor were they chary about protesting what they viewed as invasions of their rights, as witness their many petitions for redress.

Even in the area of religion, they maintained their independence. Although by 1700 they were Christians, for most of the period under discussion they chose their ministers from among their own ranks. When white ministers served, as in the case of Gideon Hawley, they often ignored their advice. And they were not averse to removing a pastor who strayed too far from the fold.

During this early period, the colony of Massachusetts established a number of governmental forms to which the Mashpees adjusted or which they opposed or ignored. Whether the Mashpees were denominated as a plantation, parish, or district was of little importance, except perhaps to the legally minded Bostonians. Mashpee ended the period largely as it had entered it, as a self-sufficient, self-governing community. Along with the colonies, the Mashpees had undergone the trauma of two colonial wars. Although they had suffered grievous losses, they had emerged from these conflicts with well-defined social and territorial boundaries and an ongoing political structure. The Mashpees, in the postrevolutionary period, had established political continuity and a stable social and economic system. The same cannot be said for their non-Indian neighbors.

❖ 5 ❖

FROM INDIAN DISTRICT
TO INDIAN TOWN

WHEN PRESIDENT JAMES MON-
ROE commissioned the Rev-
erend Jedidiah Morse to undertake a review of the Indians in
the eastern half of the United States, the government was mo-
tivated by more than benign curiosity. Under Secretary of War
John C. Calhoun the federal government was contemplating
a policy shift that would result in the removal of all Indians
from the East to land west of the Mississippi River. Morse was
one of the leading proponents of this scheme. The tour had
been proposed by Morse with the object, in Calhoun's words,
of acquiring "a more accurate knowledge of their actual condition, and to devise the most suitable plan to advance their
civilization and happiness" (Morse 1822:11). For many tribes
that progress was impeded, so the argument went, by disrepu-
table whites who associated with Indians and undid by example the Christian teachings of their ministers. This situation
could be avoided by moving the Indians to safe havens in the
West, thus giving them the time needed to learn Christian
ways. Morse was admirably suited for the purpose of advo-
cating civilization through removal because he was a minister
and a member of the Society for the Propagation of the Christian Faith and a longtime "expert" on Indian affairs.

Morse did not go to Mashpee but instead relied on a set of responses sent to him by Phineas Fish, a fellow clergyman. Fish reported that the Mashpees "have altogether adopted the habits of civilized life, of course, have forgotten their ancient names, and indeed their language also, with the exception of a very few individuals, who retain a slight knowledge of it, and are able to converse a little" (ibid.:69). He found the number of "pure-blooded" Indians small, 50 to 60 out of a population of 320. Given the long history of contact, this number might be considered large, but Fish had no inclination to ascertain an accurate figure so the estimate is questionable. The state of morality, according to Fish, was low, intemperance high, and illiteracy common, although the plantation provided and paid for a school. Though hardly supportive of the Mashpees, or even very knowledgeable about them, Fish was convinced that they would not willingly abandon their land and move west, nor was he sure that the idea had merit from the government's point of view. He wrote:

> As to the plan of removing them, were they in favor of the measure, it would scarcely be an object. They are of public utility here, as expert whalemen and manufacturers of various light articles; have lost sympathy with their brethren of the forest; are in possession of many privileges peculiar to a coast, indented by the sea; their local attachments are strong; they are tenacious of their lands, of course, the idea of alienating them and removing to a distance, would be very unpopular. This is evident from the feeling manifested by those whom I have sounded on the subject; I have reason, therefore, to believe the scheme would not take with them. (Ibid.:70)

Fish's observations concerning Mashpees' sense of independence, love of their land, and willingness to challenge authority when they felt threatened were certainly on the mark, as he was soon to find out, to his sorrow. Unhappy with what the tribal members considered to be dereliction on the part of the overseers, they filed complaints in the legislature, seeking changes in the government system. In 1827, a committee of the legislature reported that the tribe had managed its affairs for more than a century, but in recent years its leaders had been reluctant to act, in part because of problems with the overseers and in part because of divisions within the tribe. As a consequence, the tribe had been exposd to "injuries without any means of redress" (Massachusetts House of Representatives 1827:68–69). Unable to resolve the disputes with the overseers, the tribal leaders had taken it upon themselves to ignore the trustees and had evolved their own system of tribal management. "In respect to their municipal affairs," the committee reported, "the Indians have in the meantime assumed the business of self-government, and they now hold in their respective meeting houses or school houses, 'town meetings,' in which one of their own number presides; and in which they choose a Clerk, Overseer of the Poor, etc., and audit with perfect regularity and with sufficient intelligence all the accounts of their tribe" (ibid.). The committee gave tacit endorsement to the tribe's system of governance.

The state legislature took no action on the committee report, and matters remained in a quiet if nebulous state until the early 1830s, when the overseers took steps to reassert their control. This time the Mashpees did more than complain. They sent a resolution to the governor and the legislature outlining their grievances and threatening action if the abuses did not stop. In the words of the tribe:

Resolved: That we as a tribe will rule ourselves, and have the right so to do for all men are born free and Equal says the Constitution of the Country.

Resolved: That we will not permit any white man to come upon our Plantation to cut or carry off any wood or hay or any other article without our permission after the first of July next.

Resolved: That we will put said Resolution in force after that date July next with the penalty of binding and throw-

ing them from the Plantation. If they will not stay away
without. (Massachusetts Senate 1834 Doc. No. 14:5)

The memorial was signed by 102 members of the tribe,
including the president, Ebenezer Attaquin, the secretary, Israel Amos, and the deacon of the church, Isaac Coombs. The
legislative committee to which the memorial was referred expressed disbelief in the allegations but recommended that a
representative be sent to investigate (ibid.:9). Accordingly, Jo-
siah Fiske was appointed, but before he departed on his journey he received instructions from Lieutenant Governor Levi
Lincoln that made an impartial investigation impossible. Lincoln told him:

> The Indians must be made to understand their relation
> to the Government of the State, and the indispensable ne-
> cessity of requiring their peaceable obedience to the Laws.
> The misrepresentations and evil instigations by which they
> have been influenced, must be exposed, and the conse-
> quences of attempting to carry their threats into execu-
> tion, distinctly and intelligently pointed out. Let them be
> convinced, if possible, that their grievances (real or sup-
> posed) will be inquired into, and a generous and parental
> regard be had to their condition; but that disorder and
> resistance to any rightful control over their property by
> the Guardians appointed by Law, will be promptly and
> severely punished. If there should be any seditious or
> riotous proceedings, let the ringleaders be arrested and
> delivered over to the civil power. (Ibid.:13–14)

Fiske left for Mashpee on June 30 and on his arrival found
that the Mashpees had organized a new government five days
earlier and barred all whites from the reservation (ibid.:17–18).
They had fired Reverend Fish and had ordered him to leave
the plantation, and they had sent their newly appointed sher-
iff to serve notices on the overseers and treasurer, demanding
that they surrender all notes, monies, and records. The overseers refused, and the Mashpees took steps to seize the church

property. To enforce their new rules, a group led by William Apes, a Pequot Indian by birth and a Mashpee by adoption, stationed itself so as to intercept any whites attempting to remove wood. Apes had only recently come into the community and, upon seeing the conditions and observing the behavior of the white minister, had taken over the ministerial chores. His life epitomized the plight of the Mashpees and other New England tribes, and he threw himself into the conflict with considerable zeal and courage.

Born in Connecticut in 1798, William Apes had been abandoned by his parents at the age of five and left in the care of an alcoholic grandfather, who beat him unmercifully. After his injuries healed, he was "bound out" to a white family who were strict Baptists. After enduring their abuse for several years, he ran away but was quickly captured and returned to the family, who sold his indenture to a Presbyterian family. The change in denomination brought no improvement in his living conditions, yet he stayed four years, at which time he ran away again, this time to New York. Fearful that he would be caught and returned, he joined the army and was sent to Plattsburgh, where he served during the War of 1812. After the war, he was mustered out, defrauded out of his pay, and left destitute. He stayed a short time with the Mohawks at St. Regis and then returned to Connecticut. He was twenty by this time, with a lifetime of experiences. Shortly after his return to Connecticut, he received the "call" and began preaching. His brand of Protestantism was too radical for his white neighbors, and they subjected him to continual abuse. Gradually, he worked his way back into Pequot society, modified his religious views, married, and by age thirty-one became an ordained Methodist minister. It was at this juncture in his life that he met the Mashpees (Campisi 1979:v–x).

Apes and his companions did not have long to wait for a confrontation, for shortly after the Mashpees had taken up stations to interdict any removal, the first wagons arrived. "Apes, as soon as the teamsters arrived, forbade them to do anything towards the removal of wood; and as soon as one of the wagons was loaded, ordered the same to be immediately unloaded by his assistants; and while two of his number stood near him as aids, with clubs in their hands, six others, in defiance of the laws of the land, proceeded forthwith to execute the orders, and to drive the whole concern from the territory. Such was the state of things on the first day of July" (Apes 1979:10).

Commissioner Fiske reached the Cape shortly after the interception of the teamsters. He met with the minister and the overseers and decided to hold a public meeting of all the proprietors, some 229, on the afternoon of July 3. In the meantime, he inspected the books of the overseers and treasurer "in order to become minutely acquainted with the history of the Mashpee Indians, and to be the better enabled to judge in such matters" (ibid.:20).

On July 3, he met with the Mashpees at their meetinghouse. He arrived without the overseers, but the Mashpees insisted upon their presence and they were summoned. Fiske read his orders as well as the directions given to him by the governor. Apes and the other leaders remained adamant and Fiske, perceiving no change in attitude, had the leaders arrested for their actions on the first of July. Apes was required to post a $200 bond, which was provided by a white neighbor, much to the dismay of the supporters of the overseers (ibid.:38).

The arrest of Apes and two others quieted matters but did not dissipate tribal resolve. Fiske received a detailed list of grievances, which he investigated. He traveled around the plantation noting that many occupied frame houses, some thirty or so families had livestock, and a number tilled a few acres. In addition to the meetinghouse and church, there were two schoolhouses. In general, he considered the people well off. The Mashpees, by contrast, saw their conditions as deplorable. To Fiske, the problem did not rest upon the lack of a comfortable existence, "as it is for want of an unrestrained liberty and freedom from the controlling influence of government" (Massachusetts Senate 1833, Doc. 18:29). In the end, Fiske charged the problem up to misunderstandings between the Mashpees and the overseers. He found the overseers guilty of no improprieties, nor did he recommend any changes in governance (ibid.:33).

Others took up the cudgel on behalf of the Mashpees. William Lloyd Garrison wrote editorials in the *Liberator* in support of their plea for self-government (Apes 1979:89–93), and Benjamin Hallett, acting as counsel for the Mashpees, brought their case to the court and legislative bodies (Hallett 1834). After a year of controversy, in March 1834 the Senate and House of Representatives of the state of Massachusetts incorporated Mashpee as an Indian District "With all the powers and privileges, and subject to all the duties and liabilities herein provided, and necessary to carry into full effect the provisions of this act" (ARM Act of 1834, chap. 166:231). The act provided for the appointment of a commissioner to supervise tribal affairs and set the time of the first meeting at which the proprietors were to elect their officers. Elections were to be held annually in March or April at which time the Mashpees were to elect three selectmen, a clerk, and one or more constables. The selectmen were responsible for the management of all tribal property and were empowered to make any laws necessary to carry out their duties. The governor reported in his message to the legislature that the act had been properly implemented and "that harmony has prevailed, that the officers, who are Indian proprietors, were chosen with as much unanimity as is generally found in town meetings, and the provisions of the law, though their efficacy has not been fairly tested, seem thus far to be quite satisfactory" (Governor's Address 1835:64). The act culminated fifty years of struggle by Mashpee leaders to establish in law what was evident in fact.

Charles Marston, a local attorney, was appointed as the commissioner and, pursuant to the law, called a meeting of proprietors in the spring of 1834 to elect tribal officials to replace the tribal president and secretary. There were sixty eligible voters of whom fifty were present. They elected Isaac Coombs, Israel Amos, and Ezra Attaquin as selectmen, Daniel B. Amos as clerk, and Oakes A. Coombs and Jeremiah Squib as constables. The selectmen then prepared regulations to govern the taking of herring, and the proprietors voted their approval. On May 26 the commissioner called another meeting to appoint fence viewers, pass regulations governing the cutting of wood, and determine the status of the meetinghouse. The proprietors rejected the first proposal, acted on the second, and entered into a lengthy discussion on the meetinghouse before rejecting the proposed rules (Massachusetts Senate 1835 Doc. No. 8:6–7). The report gives no clue as to the changes under discussion.

The selectmen had other matters to resolve. The district contained considerable marshland and meadows, which had to be allocated. Every proprietor who had any livestock was given an equal portion of the land — called a gift share — from which to remove hay. The remainder was then leased, with the proprietors getting first choice. Any lands left were leased to neighboring whites. The same procedure was followed to allocate the tribal meadows (ibid.:7). In addition, the selectmen were required to survey the boundary between Mashpee and the town of Sandwich and settle some land disputes within the district between non-Mashpees and the tribe. By far the most difficult problem related to determining the boundaries of the private lots of the proprietors. The 1834 act establishing the district had confirmed to each proprietor the land he had appropriated. With the rejection of a fence viewer — an individual assigned the responsibility of establishing the property lines — the task fell to the selectmen and the commissioner, who reported that "No permanent record has yet been made, but plots and minutes of many of the lots have been taken preparatory to making a permanent record" (ibid.:8).

There remained the problem of Mr. Phineas Fish and the control of the parsonage. Fish adamantly refused to leave the building or relinquish control over the four hundred acres that went with it. The Mashpees instituted legal action to assure tribal title to the land (Hallett 1834) and petitioned Harvard College, which administered a bequest that financed the missionary activity (Harvard University 1836:425), to cease its support of Fish. A committee was appointed, and in time it reported on three alternatives available to the trustees. They could declare the efforts of Fish to have failed and withdraw the funds for his support. They could recognize that a large portion of the tribe did not attend his instructions, but some few did, and therefore the funds should be continued. Finally, they could divide the funds and give a part to the tribal government for religious purposes and the remainder to Fish (ibid.: 432). This recommendation was adopted and Fish's share was cut in half, the other half going to the treasurer of the Indian District. The funds distributed represented two-thirds of the income of a perpetual trust established by the Reverend Daniel Williams in the eighteenth century. The tribe employed a minister and teacher but still was prevented from using the church facilities (Harvard College Papers 1838).

Inevitably, the controversy over the use and control of the meetinghouse reached the legislature, which referred the matter to a joint special committee (Massachusetts House Reports 1839, Doc. No. 72). The committee made a thorough review of the evidence, held hearings, and recommended a compromise that allowed both groups use of the premises. It was a face-saving proposal. They found that Fish had twenty-four members in his congregation, only one of whom was an Indian—the rest were whites. E. G. Perry, the missionary and teacher hired by the Mashpees, had 202 members attending, in addition to twenty-three blacks and four whites. The committee reported "that the meetinghouse was used almost exclusively for the whites. It is proper to state that there was no obstruction to the Indians occupying seats, other than what arises from a sense of inferiority pressed upon them, of which the Indians complain" (ibid.:7). The issue was resolved in 1840, when the legislature invested the district of Mashpee "with all the powers and privileges and made subject to all the duties and liabilities, which parishes or religious societies possess . . . and the meetings of the proprietors of said district, for parish purposes, shall be called in the same manner as the meetings of the said proprietors are or may be called" (ARM 1840, chap. 65:210–11). Voting in parish meetings was limited to proprietors. Fish was allowed to use the parish during the course of his tenure at Mashpee, but the district held title to the property. In the course of this struggle, the Mashpees changed their religious affiliation to Baptist.

The dust had barely settled from the battle for control of the parsonage when the legislature passed a law to partition the land held in common and divide it among the proprietors (ibid. chap. 72:522–27). This act, though confirming title, departed little from established practice. It provided that individual proprietors would have "all the incidents of estates in fee, except the right of transfer, conveyance, or devise to other than a proprietor" (ibid.:525). Land not divided among the proprietors was to remain in common holding of the tribe. There is no legislative history for this act, and one can only surmise that it was passed to protect the proprietors' improvements to the lands they held by common agreement.

In the period from 1842 to 1870, the Mashpees exercised the functions of a tribe through the legal agency of a district. They elected selectmen annually, held tribal meetings, promulgated and enforced rules, maintained order, provided education, and took care of the poor and indigent. A report of the commissioners in 1849 set the native population at 279, most of whom were involved in subsistence agriculture. The report reflects the ambiguities concerning Indians so prevalent in mid-nineteenth-century America; on one hand, they were seen as a self-sufficient people living in comfortable surroundings; on the other, they were depicted as deficient in their development toward civilization. Both views appeared in the same paragraph:

> The larger portion of the tribe secure a tolerably comfortable living; quite a number are poor and improvident, eking out a scanty support by begging. They are behind the tribes already considered in the social arts and domestic comforts; none reaching the conditions of the best, very many falling below the worst. The majority live in comfortable framed houses, while many still occupy huts and hovels, amidst filth and degradation. As to chastity

and temperance too, they are behind the other tribes, though the uniform testimony is, that in both these respects, particularly in regard to temperance, there have been great improvements during the last 15 or 20 years. (Massachusetts House of Representatives 1849, Doc. No. 46:25)

According to the report, the Indian District had cost the commonwealth the inordinate amount of $2,155.42 from 1843 through 1848. "The amount, it is true, is somewhat large," wrote the commissioners, "still, under the operation of elevating influences which we do not despair of seeing brought to bear upon this people, they become capable of self-support, every consideration of humanity and of policy even, requires the adoption of a generous treatment" (ibid.:29). The commission held that the expenditures for indigents were justified because, it argued, alcoholism was the cause of the indigence, "as the white man has introduced the sole cause of pauperism, he should provide liberally for the result" (ibid.:30).

In general, the commission found the District Act of 1834 had had a beneficial effect on the Mashpees and that their conditions had improved with greater self-government. As a portent of things to come, the commission expressed the conviction that, with proper guidance, the Mashpees would soon be ready for "complete civil and political enfranchisement. In a few years, the district of Mashpee may claim a place by the side of the other towns of the Commonwealth" (ibid.:38). In 1853, the office of commissioner was abolished, its duties transferred to a treasurer, and the remainder of its powers and responsibilities to the Indian selectmen (ARM Acts of 1852–53, chap. 186:466–68). A House of Representatives report pronounced that "the inhabitants of Mashpee are now well satisfied with their civil privileges, and desire no further present change in this respect, unless it be the right to nominate their Treasurer; and it will be apparent, from this brief epitome of their civil history, that they form an interesting community" (Massachusetts House of Representatives 1855, Doc. No. 192:5).

In 1859, the Massachusetts Senate appointed John Milton Earle to conduct yet another investigation of Mashpee. His report, submitted in 1861, provides the most complete census data available up to that time (Massachusetts Senate 1861, Doc. No. 96:xx–xxxvii). According to the report, there were 371 Mashpees and 32 non-Mashpees living in the district. The predominant occupation was that of mariner or seaman, with farmer second. He concluded that the large number of absent men and the low level of agricultural development were caused by geographical factors. "The natural poverty of the soil, and this comparative isolation precludes them from obtaining profitable employment at home, and almost drives the men to a seafaring life, as a means of subsistence" (ibid.:63).

The Mashpee District contained more than sixteen thousand acres distributed as follows:

Indian lands held in severalty	10,231.5	
Indian lands (upland), in common	2,300.5	
Indian lands, Parsonage	450.0	
Indian lands, Cedar Swamps	250.0	
Indian lands, salt and fresh meadows	150.0	
Total Indian lands		13,382
Mashpee and Wakeby ponds	850.0	
John's Pond	350.0	
Cotuit, or Santuit Pond	250.0	
Ashumets Pond	200.0	
Total large ponds		1,650
Lands held by whites, estimated	700.0	
Roads, rivers, and small ponds	400.0	
Total lands held by whites, roads, rivers, and small ponds		1,100
Total whole area		16,132

(Ibid.:48)

The transfer of the ownership of the wood from public to private was especially disturbing, according to Earle, because it reduced the revenue available to the tribe. "Relying on the sale of their wood, to procure whatever they might want, agriculture was neglected, idle and improvident habits were acquired, and a general unthriftiness ensued that pervaded the whole District" (ibid.:49).

Earle acknowledged that another source of revenue was available to the tribe — taxation — but he found this unenforceable: "The Act of 1842 empowers the proprietors to assess taxes for the purposes of the District, but the provision is practically nugatory, for the want of power to enforce their collection. The experiment when tried, has utterly failed and had to be abandoned" (ibid.:53). Earle recognized the dilemma inherent in commonwealth policy; existing law provided no means to collect the taxes, but any change in the law that would empower the collection would have to be based on the ability to alienate the land. As Earle stated it:

> But it is not seen how it [collection of taxes] could be exercised, consistently with the settled policy of the State in reference to the Indians, as, by existing laws, none of the territory could be alienated and pass into the hands of others than proprietors, and there are now, hundreds, if not thousands of acres of land in the District, which could be bought for a price almost nominal, yet find no purchaser, because such proprietors as are able to buy, already hold in severalty more land than they have any occasion for. There would, consequently, be no purchasers. If provision were made that others might become purchasers, it would initiate a vital change in the policy of the State, and lead to a gradual, but certain alienation of a considerable portion of the lands of the tribe, whose owners would, probably, in that event, be thrown upon the public for support. (Ibid.:53–54)

Earle captured the dilemma of public policy toward Indians: the conflicting values and motives that permeated white-Mashpee relationships and intruded upon the functioning of tribal society. To "civilize" the Mashpees was to risk the exploitation and alienation of their land, but to continue the commonwealth guardianship was to deny them full benefits as citizens and burden the treasury of the state. Increasing their internal autonomy, in this view, endangered their land base, but leaving the ownership of the land in the hands of the tribe went contrary to the commonly held beliefs of the relationship between industry, progress, and private property. Although it is of small comfort, this intellectual conundrum was not unique to Massachusetts, for this scenario was played out with many tribes across the continent.

The legislature did not wait long to act, and when it did, it reflected its ambivalence. In 1862, it extended civil rights to all Indians not members of the Mashpee and several other specified tribes, but it permitted members of these tribes to become citizens by certifying and paying a poll tax (ARM Act of 1862, chap. 184:149–51). The following year the legislature granted the Mashpees the right to choose their treasurer, who could be either a proprietor or a nonmember white (ibid., Act of 1863, chap. 183:494–95). In 1864, the tribe was given greater control over its fisheries, and the prosecution of violators of tribal rules was made the responsibility of the county (ibid., Act of 1864, chap. 150:91–92). Thus it moved in opposite directions, toward assimilation and tribal autonomy.

At the end of the decade, the two major issues facing the Mashpees and the commonwealth remained unresolved: the extension of full citizenship and the right of unlimited alienation of the land. To address these issues, the legislature authorized the Committee on Indians to hold hearings at Mashpee. Sentiments were divided. One group, led by Matthias Amos, favored the propositions, seeing little adverse effect and doubting that any sizable portion of the land would be alienated. He acknowledged that land values would rise and new capital would be brought into the community (Massachusetts House of Representatives 1869, Doc. No. 502:10–12). It is interesting that a few years previous to this Amos, along with Solomon Attaquin and Oakes A. Coombs, had been granted a corporate charter to establish a manufacturing company in Mashpee (ARM Act of 1866–67, chap. 41:491–92). William Simons spoke in opposition to the removal of the entailment. He told the members of the committee, "I don't think we are able to have this entailment come off yet. I feel it would be a great disadvantage to us as a body. Our land would go the same as our wood has gone. We have some privileges that might be improved if we had the capital to work them with, but we have not got a dollar and taking the entailment off will not fetch it there, only from outside people, and if outside men come on to make improvements, they fetch outside help" (ibid.:16).

The venerable Blind Joe Amos, long the spiritual leader of the Mashpees, lent his voice to those who opposed the removal of the restrictions on the alienation of the land:

> Looking at the opportunities we have had, and what we would need before we would be ready, I have come to this conclusion, knowing and believing that the time would come, when the honorable legislature of this State would take away the entailments upon our properties, and would place us upon the ground of equal rights — take away all the restrictions, and make us in every respect in that matter, like other men. That I look for — that I am looking for now. It was not with opposition against that proceeding that we remonstrated against the petition, but it is my view, when I say we are not ready for it now. I think there is a lack of education, though there has been a great many improvements made, and to a large extent. It is almost surprising to see the difference there is now in the people of Marshpee, within the twenty years that is past and gone, yet I believe that the reason which I render, that we are not ready for it, is true. It was stated, when we were placed under these restrictions, and the entailment was placed upon our properties, that it was because we were not capable of taking care of it, and the white man, the foreigner from anywhere, would be likely to get away from us our properties, because they had more understanding; they were more shrewd, and knew better how to use themselves. (Ibid.:18)

Others spoke in support of the concept, stressing the ability of the Mashpees to administer their affairs like any community and provide necessary services. The opposition centered on entailment, not suffrage, although the state had inextricably linked the two.

The state of Massachusetts was reacting to a number of motives, some manifest and others not. In responding to a petition from some of the proprietors, the legislative committee had received encouragement from the governor, who, in his annual message to the legislature, had pointed out the inconsistency of a policy that gave "equal civil and political rights to all citizens" (Massachusetts House of Representatives 1869, Doc. No. 438:1) but denied them to Indians. "There are, scattered over the State, more than one thousand of our people called Indians, who are placed under partial civil disabilities, and who are politically disenfranchised. They are not paupers, or slaves, and yet not citizens. They are treated as the wards of the Commonwealth, recipients of its charities, but debarred from all agency in making the laws by which they are governed. It is unnecessary to enlarge upon the reasons why this political anomaly should so long have existed in this Commonwealth. It should exist no longer" (ibid.).

The governor's words were not to imply that the extension of political equality meant that he believed in social equality. The Indians labored under a disability that "has been to increase and perpetuate their incapacity for citizenship," the cure for which was "to place upon them all its responsibilities" (ibid.:2). The object was to merge them into the general society.

Implicit in the committee's report is the view that the existing situation fostered "pauperism" and a burden of expense to be borne by the commonwealth. The generosity of the commonwealth in providing for the indigent and the inability of the Indians to sell their lands and seek their fortunes elsewhere were the principal factors retarding their progress toward "civilization." In a fine display of fence straddling, the committee was able to find enough pauperism, abetted by government dole, to support the view that the Indians had not measured up, but not enough to act as an impediment to their enfranchisement.

In a passage that gives insight into the thinking of the legislature, the committee wrote:

> We are called upon in Massachusetts to solve, upon a
> small scale, the problem which has so long perplexed, and
> which today perplexes our national councils. In the treat-
> ment of the American Indian our government has tried
> everything but justice. The Slave Power dictated our In-
> dian policy, and the result has been generations of bloody
> war, frightful waste of public treasure and chronic war.
> The simple solution of this whole problem has all the while
> lain in that one noble utterance of President Grant, in his
> inaugural address — citizenship for the Indian. Let him
> fulfill the promise of that one work, and when the laurels
> of the military chieftain fade, the glories of that achieve-
> ment of Christian statesmanship will be immortal. (Ibid.:
> 12)

Bolstered by this patriotic verve and sustained by their Christian beliefs in the nature of human progress toward civilization as it could only be revealed to and by a believer, the committee recommended several acts to remove what it perceived as "disabilities." It proposed the enfranchisement of all Indians in Massachusetts because, as it explained, "The fifteenth article of amendment to the Constitution of the United States, will, when duly ratified, prohibit the denial or abridgement of the right to vote on account of color or race; but other disabilities will still attach to the Indians of this Commonwealth, and the purpose of this act is to remove them all" (ibid.:14). Accordingly, Indians were to be granted citizenship and the entailment of their land removed (ibid.). In addition to these general provisions, the committee recommended a special act for Mashpee. Though such a choice was not favored by the Mashpees, a majority of the committee recommended that the Indian District be incorporated as a town and the judge probate be empowered to divide up and sell the common lands (ibid.:15). The legislature dutifully complied and in 1869 granted citizenship and divided the land in fee simple (ARM Act of

1869, chap. 463:780). In 1870, it abolished the district and incorporated the town (ibid. Act of 1870, chap. 293:213–15).

The acts that granted citizenship and suffrage and established the town did not abolish the tribe. The tribe, which had governed the Indian District, now governed the town, the selectmen of the Indian District became the selectmen of the town, and the issues handled by the political organization of the tribe under the town form of government were essentially the same as those handled when it was a district.

If anything, the establishment of the town expanded the Mashpees' political invovlement and control by making more positions available to them. The Mashpees not only held a virtual monopoly over the positions of selectman but also those of town clerk, tax collector, treasurer, and constable.

Earle's admonition in the 1861 report that converting Mashpee to a town would result in the loss of tribal control of the land became a reality very soon after the passage of the 1869 and 1870 acts. In April 1871 the commissioners appointed for the purpose by the Superior Court divided the common lands, some 2,536.25 acres, into 187 lots and sold them for an aggregate sum of $7,056.76. The money was turned over to the town. For their services the three commissioners received $17,267.00 (Massachusetts Senate 1878, Doc. No. 238:2–11) from the treasury of the commonwealth. In addition to the sale of the common lands, the land held privately by Mashpees quickly became owned by non-Mashpees. By the 1930s, over half the total land of the former plantation was alienated by Mashpee Indians (Zimmerman 1938).

The alienation of the land did not result in any change in the political system of the town. The Mashpees continued to dominate political affairs because most of the non-Mashpees who purchased land remained absentee owners, providing tax dollars for the support of the community but not participating in its political affairs.

Mashpee continued as an isolated Indian community, recognized as such by the legislature and local historians and in news reports. The following selection illustrates both the remoteness of the tribe and the tendency to describe it in picturesque if condescending terms:

> Mashpee comes upon the traveller like a surprise. It lies in ambush, as it were, and is discovered only after careful searching. Instead of following the pattern of the new England village, with its one main street bordered by white houses with green blinds, its church with tall spire and its shaded common, Mashpee is settled without regular design, with pink, grey, and yellow houses set among the forest trees. . . . Since their determined settling among the Cape Cod colonists, the Friendly Indians have followed, as far as possible, the occupations of the whites, formerly in sharing the whaling voyages, and latterly in farming and cranberry-picking. To these occupations they have added the more distinctly Indian pursuits of manufacturing baskets and brooms and peddling these wares with berries and fish. The wandering life of the hunter and fisher has been most congenial to the Mashpee Indians, and acting the idler has been always carried on in spite of the example of the industrious Cape Cod people of the neighborhood. (*New England Magazine* 1890:278–79)

Another observer, Rosamond Rothery, reflected more favorably on the sylvan nature of Mashpee, referring to it as a forgotten corner of the Cape, where "no one hurries: indeed, how could one? There is no bustling square; no crowded marketplace; no rival church with clanging bells to split the wide tranquility; no flying to catch the train, for there is no train, soiling the blue with a smoky pennant" (1918:238). Notwithstanding the evident romanticism and nostalgia of the passages, it is clear that Mashpee reflected a unique character, its residents a homogeneous group with their own value system, admired by few and deplored by many, and its own social and political networks. This tribal community, regardless of the specific statutes under which it operated, persisted by virtue of its social and geographical isolation and because of a strong tendency for intragroup marriage. Legally, membership in the town was defined by residency, but for all practical purposes access to political power and social prestige depended on being recognized as a member by birth of one of the several lineages that traced their descent at least to 1859 and, in some cases, further back. The legal transformations of the century did little to alter the insularity of the community or disrupt the native political processes. It would take another half-century or more for the effects of the town's incorporation to become evident.

❖ 6 ❖

ADJUSTING TO CHANGE

THE TRANSITION from Indian District to incorporated town had little political impact on Mashpee in the years immediately following the change. The last three selectmen of the Indian District—Silas Pells, Walter Mingo, and Solomon Attaquin—became the first three selectmen of the town. The district regulations governing the taking of clams, oysters, and herring, the cutting of wood and grass, and the leasing of fishing rights along the streams and rivers became, without interruption, the laws of the town. As the Mashpees had controlled the political offices of the district, so they elected or appointed Mashpees to every one of the town offices. In the course of the next sixty years, all but one of the thirty-one selectmen were Mashpees or persons related by marriage to Mashpees. The Mashpees held every other position in town government, the appointees being drawn from a core of families that dominated Mashpee politics. Yet this stability belied three important changes that were occurring within the community. On the economic level, the Mashpees were losing title to their land; politically, they were divided into parties—Republican and Democrat—and linked, if tenuously, to the county, state, and national political structures; culturally, they were undergoing a revitalization movement.

Until 1842 the tribe had held title to all the land in Mashpee with the exception of a few small grants to outsiders. Individual proprietors possessed a transferable use right and the right to sell any improvements made on the land. In 1842, the legislature passed a law requiring the partitioning of the land with individual Mashpees having "all the incidents in fee, except the right of transfer, conveyance, or devise to other than a proprietor" (ARM Act of 1842, chap. 72:523–27). Although the act vested title in the individual, the restriction on sale or transfer depressed land values and sharply restricted sales. Most of the land of the town was divided among the proprietors with the tribe retaining some two thousand acres of common land and the rights along the streams and rivers. The acts of 1869 and 1870 removed the restriction on private sales (ibid. Act of 1869, chap. 463:780–82) and authorized the sale of the common lands by the court (ibid. Act of 1870, chap. 293:90–91). The court soon ordered the division and sale of the tribally owned land, and private individuals purchased large sections of the woodlands, bogs, and shorefront properties. According to Carle Zimmerman, in 1871 48 nonresidents owned 11 percent of the land in the town; by 1934, 666 nonresidents owned 86 percent (1938:169). Equally dramatic was the shift in valuation. By 1900 more than half the taxes were being paid by nonresidents and by 1920 nonresidents paid four times as many taxes as residents. This shift was not just the function of the exchange of existing land values or the increase of value because of construction. Through their control of the political system, the Mashpees were able to grant tribal members tax advantages through reduced assessments, abatements, and exemptions. Zimmerman provides the following example:

> In this case, the head of the household receives a salary from the communal town funds which enables him to live very well. His mother-in-law, a widow 80 years old, lives with him. She owns some property in the community, but is exempt from taxes because of her age and because she is a widow. Her son lives on this piece of property and

gets free rent plus support from the town treasury; he
pays only a poll tax, and evades any tax on the property
on which he lives. This large family with its complicated
arrangements is communal in that it takes care of each
member in one way or another, but it is individualized
when it comes to avoiding responsibilities — such as tax-
paying. It should really be called a clan because 15 out
of 189 voters listed in 1934 bear its name, and it is closely
intermarried with other groups casting as many as 30 percent of the total community votes at the tribal council.
This story could be retold a number of times as a domi-
nant family pattern for the community. (Ibid.:177)

Taxing nonresidents disproportionately to support the activities and needs of town residents was not invented by the
Mashpees; it was a common feature of most communities with
a summer population. But in the instance of the Mashpees,
when the state of Massachusetts unilaterally created a town
out of an Indian district, it imbued the tribe with powers it
exercised for the benefit of tribal members who were coincidentally town members. Access to political power and thereby
to town resources was dependent on being a member of the
Mashpee tribe; however, there would have been no resources
available without the act permitting the alienation of the land
and without the subsequent sales. Had the town been in a less
remote area, one closer, for example, to an industrial center,
there would have been greater occupation by non-Mashpees
with the attendant loss of political control, as occurred in other
New England Indian communities such as Narragansett, Western Abenaki, Pequot, and Schaghticoke. The result would
then have been, in all likelihood, the establishment of an Indian community living with but separate from the majority
of non-Indians. This did not occur in Mashpee. Instead, the
Mashpees (like the Gay Head tribe on Martha's Vineyard) capi-
talized on the newly available resources — tax base and political power — to develop a unique adaptation.

One of the results of this adaptation was the development
of political parties. From the 1870s on, the Mashpees were at

least nominally Republican, although they appeared to have little to do with state or national politics. In 1885, Watson F. Hammond, a longtime leader of the Mashpees, was elected to a term in the Massachusetts General Court (*Barnstable Patriot,* Jan. 5, 1886:2), but this was not a remarkable political achievement because it appears that the position was rotated among the towns that made up the election district (Soper 1890:278).

Throughout the nineteenth century and the early decades of the twentieth, political power had moved, almost as a matter of succession, through a limited number of families. The three most prominent were the Attaquin, Coombs, and Amos. By the early 1900s, the Attaquin name ceased to appear in the records and the Coombs name appeared less frequently. The Amos family, however, maintained continuous involvement in tribal politics. Israel Amos, the brother of the preacher Blind Joe Amos was one of the first district selectmen. Later, his two sons, Matthias and Daniel, served as selectmen; Matthias continued to hold office after the formation of the town. His son Horatio and grandson Lysander followed the tradition, which culminated with Matthias's great-grandson Edmund B. Amos succeeding to the office of selectman. It was "Eddie" Amos who finally merged the kinship-based political system with the political party structure. One elderly lifelong resident saw the two facets — family and Republican party membership — as one and the same. "When I was a kid they were all Republicans and except for one or two people the Republicans used to take every vote — not that so many people bothered to vote. You got to remember we were pretty much alone and it was mostly the selectmen that ran the show. They knew the people up in the county so it paid to be a Republican" (Campisi 1977).

Edmund B. Amos was born in 1887 and at the age of twenty-two was appointed to his first public office on the school committee, a position from which he promptly resigned. In 1911, he was appointed to a three-year term on the cemetery committee. Two years later he became the sealer of weights and measures, a position he held until 1918. He was a fire warden from 1914 to 1917, and in 1915 he became town treasurer, a position he held without interruption until 1927. In 1921 he was elected selectman and continued in that office until his defeat in 1927 (TR 1909–28). According to one person, during this period, "Eddie Amos ran the show up to that point. He wanted to run the whole show and while he couldn't be more than one selectman at a time, he would just put others in. Before [Stephen A.] Peters, there wasn't any split because politics didn't amount to much. Then Peters came in and others backed him because they felt Amos was running the whole show himself" (Campisi 1977).

Amos left elected office, but his political ties had served him well; he was appointed postmaster of the town. The election of 1927, which saw the political demise of Amos, saw also the rise of a new leadership, that of Stephen A. Peters.

Peters was born in 1896. He received his public school education at New Bedford, Massachusetts, and Boston, returning to Mashpee to take up residence in 1923. He soon became involved in tribal politics, and in 1927 he challenged and defeated Eddie Amos for the position of selectman. Peters and his supporters formed the Democratic party, and with the election of 1927 they won control of town and tribe.

The Peters group had come to power in part by campaigning for rural electrification, and they promptly had electricity installed in the town. Their leadership, however, was not unanimously acclaimed, and in 1929, they were challenged by a slate led by four women representing prominent Mashpee families: Mrs. Anna Pocknett ran for library trustee; her daughter Mrs. George Avant for tax collector; Mrs. William Sturgis for town clerk; and Mrs. Ferdinand Mills for town treasurer. In addition, Harrison Frye ran for selectman against the incumbent John H. Haynes, a supporter of Peters. A reporter for the *Boston Globe* gave the following description of the issues in the election:

> Put in a nutshell, it is said to be a contest for political supremacy between "the Amos crowd" and "the Peters crowd," with the nonresident taxes as the stake. The valua-

tion of resident real and personal property is only $47,635; nonresident taxable property is valued at more than $700,000. The greater part of the township of Mashpee is assessed to Summer residents; among them is numbered President A. Lawrence Lowell of Harvard and many other persons of wealth and prestige. Only this week the sale of the woodland shore tract known as Popponessett, for more than $300,000 was announced.

Except for employment on Summer estates, or work for Town Government, financed largely by the taxes on such estates, means and modes of livelihood are scarce in Mashpee. The leading political power several years ago was Edmund Amos, who is a director of the Cape Cod Chamber of Commerce and Republican committeeman for the town. . . .

Edmund Amos, although a powerful factor in politics through his personal influence, is barred from running for office because last year when the postmastership of Mashpee fell vacant, he accepted the appointment. However, by kinship he is related to all the old families of Mashpee and whether by coincidence or not, each of the women candidates in the 1929 election belongs to a leading old Indian family. Victory for the women's ticket "would mean a reinstatement of the old clan in power." (Mar. 4, 1929:24)

Both sides conducted a heated and at times vitriolic campaign, which culminated with the annual meeting and election. When the votes were counted, the Peters group had retained political control, but its control of the tribal government was short-lived. In 1930, Harrison Frye was elected selectman and Stephen Peters left office (TR 1930:1). The economic situation of the residents took a sharp turn for the worse as the town felt the first effects of the Depression, exacerbated by its own long-standing financial problems. In April 1930, a state audit reported a shortage of $1,240.54 in the treasurer's accounts (*Boston Traveler*, Apr. 29, 1930:1). The following year the town found itself out of funds by November, with no treasurer and no authorization to borrow (*Boston Globe*, Nov. 13, 1931:37). These financial problems led to another state audit and a recommendation from the state commissioner of corporations and taxation that the legislature appoint a commission to investigate the town's financial situation and to consider the possibility of annexing Mashpee to either Falmouth or Barnstable (*Boston Traveler*, Dec. 3, 1931:14).

The state-appointed commission held hearings on the financial problems in mid-March 1932 at the Mashpee town hall. The tribe's political leaders exchanged charges: Eddie Amos, who had recently been elected town clerk while continuing as postmaster, laid the blame on those who served as selectmen since 1926 — his political foes. Stephen Peters countered that the laxity in tax collection had a long history, as had mismanagement, and that the town's problems had been blown out of proportion. Although an Amos supporter, Harrison Frye, the chairman of the Board of Selectmen, agreed with Peters. "This condition," he told the commission, "has not come in the past few months, nor past few years, but it is a condition which has occurred from time to time in the past. Our condition as a whole may appear as if we as a town cannot carry on. But I believe that it is one which can be remedied by our own town officials" (*New Bedford Evening Standard*, Mar. 17, 1932:11). He went on to argue that the tribe had already made significant improvements in the town's financial condition, but the commission was not reassured. It pointed out that the town had coming due, within the next five months, temporary notes totaling $26,000, with no apparent means to pay them.

Others addressed the commissioners, urging them to preserve the town by imposing state fiscal controls similar to ones placed on other Massachusetts towns in similar straits (*Boston Globe*, Mar. 17, 1932:2; *Boston Herald*, Mar. 19, 1932:10). Perhaps the most incisive testimony was given by Lorenzo T. Hammond, a lifetime member of the community. He identified the pernicious manner in which kinship affected tribal-town administration. "Lorenzo T. Hammond, whose Indian title is Chief Little Bear, said that things were a little different in Mashpee than they were in some of the other communities in the state, because of the strong inter-family relationship. And this was so strong, he stated, that the persons in authority did not say to their subordinates, 'this is your duty' and that they were apt to overlook cases of laxity and other acts which might be classified as crimes" (*Boston Post*, Mar. 17, 1932:10).

The commissioners, for their part, stressed that the annexation of the town was a last consideration and that they were seeking other alternatives for solving the fiscal problems (ibid.). Their position on annexation was not solely of their making. Before discussing the problems with the Mashpees, the commissioners had conducted negotiations with the neighboring towns of Falmouth, Sandwich, and Barnstable. The latter two quickly rejected the suggestion, but Falmouth initially indicated some interest (*Boston Globe*, Mar. 11, 1932:4). When the town held a public hearing to discuss the annexation, however, the selectmen and commissioners were met with unanimous opposition and the plan was dropped (*Boston Herald*, Mar. 12, 1932:6).

Stephen Peters returned to power in 1932 after a two-year absence; however, the political disputation was far from over and, in 1935, there was another challenge for tribal control. Three slates of candidates ran for office. One, led by Mabel Avant and termed the "feminist" ticket because it included five women, was in reality the Amos party. Harrison Frye, a former ally of Amos, headed the second slate, and Stephen Peters led the third (*Boston Globe*, Feb. 19, 1935:16). The campaign, like past ones, was vituperative, with result that the Peters group retained its control and Frye was reelected (TR 1935:3). By this time, Peters, in addition to being the local Democratic leader, was an inspector for the Massachusetts State Department of Agriculture (*Boston Herald*, June 3, 1936:4) and a director of a number of federal relief projects (personal communication, R. Peters 1981). Peters won again in the spring of 1936 and with other Democrats fought off a strong challenge from the Republicans, who had the support of the Republican presidential candidate, Alfred Landon. This challenge was made by yet another Mashpee leader, Ambrose Pells, the town assessor (*Boston Traveler*, Nov. 3, 1938).

The political party identifications and involvement, the "splinter groups," and the machinations of the opposing leaders give Mashpee the appearance of a community indistinguishable from other small towns. Yet the Indian ethnicity and the cohesiveness it supplied made the community's governance unique. There existed throughout the period from the organization of the town through the 1930s an informal, kin-based tribal leadership that made the important decisions for the town. Carle C. Zimmerman, a sociologist from Harvard University and a specialist in small-town research, studied a number of Massachusetts communities in the 1930s, including Mashpee, and found:

> This Tribal Council [meaning the informal tribal leadership] which is Littleville's [Mashpee] real, as distinguished from the "blueprint," government, is essentially a primary group (in the Cooley sense) with a language (and a reality) of its own. . . . Meetings are always private — understood only by the initiated. They are highly informal, the balance of power being in the hands of a dozen of the mature men of the council who have proved by experience that they can achieve the aims of the tribe.
>
> At these meetings the aims and the next objectives of the tribe are agreed upon. Then a "town meeting" is called. The town meeting is nothing more than a legal form which adds prestige to the things already agreed upon at the Tribal Council. The debates and differences of the Tribal Council are never discussed in the town meeting because this meeting is also open to non-tribal members. Perhaps a representative of the State House attends the meeting: to him they present a united front and a single conclusive line of evidence. The "social mind" which is made up at the Tribal Council comes to the town meeting without dissension. (1937:178–79)

When interviewed in 1979, Zimmerman confirmed that Littleville was indeed Mashpee and that an informal tribal council did exist; he had appeared before it when seeking permission to conduct the research (Zimmerman Mar. 26, 1979: Interview).

Zimmerman saw the Mashpees as a tribe using the offices of town government to gain access to and control of outside resources. He identified four mechanisms by which the Mashpees sought to accomplish their objectives. First, there was community solidarity based on common ancestry, history, and culture. Second, the Mashpees manifested a friendly attitude toward outsiders, and third, they maintained distinct social boundaries. Fourth, though professing ties to political parties, the Mashpees were not ideologues. They shifted their positions to suit the political climate and their perception of community needs. The behaviors described by Zimmerman were boundary-maintaining devices, adjustments to conditions over which the Mashpees had no control. Zimmerman described this "we-they" dichotomy without realizing its significance to an understanding of the community:

> In some communities income gives approximately the same differentiation of the people as does wealth. In Littleville, however, family size, political power and income are strongly correlated with each other, so that an individual may have a fairly good income and yet possess little wealth. The families with the most votes are most influential when it comes to political power, and they elect members of their clans to the best-paying positions in the town.
>
> There are differences based upon religion, family relationship and blood mixture, but these differences are all of minor significance in the larger role of the community as a cumulative group for self-protective purposes. Even the relatively wealthy depend upon the poor for their position in the community, and the poor depend upon the wealthy for their share in the community funds. As a result, social discriminations are insignificant, intermarriages are frequent, and social classes are not important. The few whites who live permanently in the town are classified as outsiders, and although they may attend the town

meetings, they are not considered part of the tribal organization. (1937:185–86)

In spite of the political divisions within the community, the objectives of the leaders and the families they represented remained constant: access to and control of outside resources. The imposition of state control over their fiscal affairs did little to alter this. A report issued in 1939 gave the following description of the economic conditions within the community. "At the present time," wrote a reporter for the *Boston Evening Transcript*, "based on a recent survey, the community's income was derived from these sources, in order of importance: town employment, charity and work relief, seasonal industries (cranberrying, fishing and hunting, employment by summer residents, part-time farming, local trade, miscellaneous). There is no full-time farmer in the town" (Kearful August 17, 1939:14). The writer noted, as had Zimmerman before him, the importance of kinship in the political process, the closeness of extended family ties, and the role of an "informal" council in decision making. His conclusions closely correspond to Zimmerman's findings earlier in the decade:

> An experience based upon a long period of State guardianship and the influence of racial differences have here produced a community thoroughly adapted to making a living by relying on outside resources. The manner of making a living makes use of several facts and principals [sic]: race and background have preserved a common interest; friendliness and courtesy are always employed in dealing with visitors and outsiders, "entangling alliances" with outsiders are avoided; political affiliations are readily shifted according to circumstances; the prestige that goes with the tradition of being an Indian community is fostered; the pseudo-initiation ceremonies to the tribe are used in gaining political affiliations; individual outside sponsors are gained who will work for their benefit: the opinion is now widely held that the people are actually unable to govern themselves and are incapable of mak-

ing a living through their own efforts: visible assets are spent while the natural resources of the town remain in reserve. (Ibid.)

Throughout most of their history the Mashpees had been isolated, not only from the neighboring non-Indian communities but also from much of American Indian society; however, by the end of the nineteenth century, two factors operated to intrude on their insularity, and this intrusion had a profound effect on their tribal development. Beginning in the early part of the twentieth century, the Mashpees underwent a cultural revitalization, sparked, in part, by the return of two men with dissimilar personalities: Eben Queppish, who had spent much of his life in wild west shows, and Nelson Drew Simons, who had been educated at the Carlisle Indian School. This movement was also ignited by a growing nostalgia among easterners concerning the Indian heritage of New England. The first factor made possible the revitalization, while the second provided support and encouragement. As added spark, the cultural revitalization coincided with a series of tricentennial celebrations that further piqued interest in the region's Indian populations. A plethora of "chiefs" and Indian "princesses" appeared in newspapers along with the establishment of a number of pan-Indian groups designed to preserve "Indian culture" and assert Indian rights.

The movement received its impetus from Nelson Drew Simons, who had returned to the community around 1914 (*Barnstable Patriot Supplement*, May 2, 1921:3). He succeeded his uncle Watson Hammond as town clerk in 1915 and claimed that on the death of Hammond, one year later, he was elected chief (ibid.). If so, it was a self-election. In 1921, while serving as postmaster, he attended a law school in Boston, completing his degree in 1925 at the age of forty (*Cape Cod Magazine*, June 1925:19). At some point he assumed an Indian name, Wabung Annung, which he translated as Morning Star. He claimed to be a descendant of the Pequot sachem Sassacus (*Barnstable Patriot Supplement*, May 2, 1921:3), and he believed that the Mashpees were Pequots (*Cape Cod Magazine*, June 1921:36).

Eben Queppish was about ten years older than Simons and had a strikingly different life history. As a boy he had joined the wild west show of Montana Charlie, where he came in contact with Indians from western tribes. Later, he became a member of Buffalo Bill Cody's troupe but left after a few seasons. He returned to the Boston area, where he worked as part of a living exhibit in an establishment called Austen and Stone's. He supplemented his income by making splint baskets, a skill he said he learned from his father. In the summer he worked as a cook at a wealthy hunting lodge near Mashpee (*Cape Cod Magazine*, Aug. 16, 1926:10), a job he kept until his death in 1933 (*New Bedford Standard Times*, Jan. 11, 1933:1-2).

Simons and Queppish were soon joined by others interested in renewing their Mashpee heritage, and by 1928 a new organization had formed — the Wampanoag Nation — combining leaders from Indian groups on and near the Cape. In October, members from Mashpee, Gay Head, and Herring Pond met at the Baptist church at Herring Pond to elect leaders of the newly formed entity. After two days of meetings, they selected the Reverend Leroy C. Perry (Pocassett), the minister to the Narragansett Indians of Rhode Island, to be supreme sachem. Perry, who took the name Ousamequin, which he translated as Yellow Feather, had been chosen as chief of the Wampanoags by a group calling itself the Indian Council of New England in 1923 (Speck 1928a:21). Eben Queppish, who called himself Red Jacket, was chosen as supreme medicine man (*Falmouth Enterprise*, Sept. 27, 1928:7; *Boston Globe*, Oct. 10, 1928:12; *New Bedford Sunday Standard*, Oct. 14, 1928:1-2). A month later Perry installed Lorenzo T. Hammond (Little Bear) as chief of the Mashpees. Lorenzo was the son of Watson Hammond and the cousin of Nelson Simons, who appears to have dropped out of the tribal picture by this time. Perry filled two additional positions: William James (High Eagle) became the Mashpee medicine man and Clinton Haynes (Wild Horse) became secretary (*New Bedford Sunday Times*, Aug. 11, 1929: 30). The last named were to figure prominently in a leadership dispute during the next decade.

In August of the following year, the new "nation" organized its first powwow. It is evident that the leadership had not coalesced and there was some shifting of roles. William James and Eben Queppish appear to have exchanged positions, with James becoming the chief medicine man and Queppish the medicine man of the Mashpees (ibid. June 28, 1929:20). Haynes became historian as well as secretary, and Clarence Wixon (Red Shell), a Mashpee, was designated sagamore or second in command (ibid. Aug. 11, 1929:30). Wixon took on a second, if unofficial, responsibility, that of publicist for the organization. He filled the local papers with articles and press releases.

The powwow was not new to Mashpee, although the form and content changed substantially after 1929. For more than two hundred years, the Mashpees had held an annual homecoming during the summer. The meetings covered several days and afforded individual tribal members who no longer lived in the community an opportunity to associate with friends and family. The occasion renewed family ties and reinforced a sense of group membership. There were family outings, clambakes on South Cape beaches, and a nearly continuous round of family visits. In time, the meetings took on more formal characteristics, particularly in the latter part of the nineteenth century, when religiously based, locally written pageants were used to teach moral concepts. One elderly resident recalled: "Every child was expected to attend the pageants and most had parts to play. The themes were about honest, Christian-living, family. And you took them serious. Sometimes there were stories depicted like 'The Great Giant,' but mostly they were moral plays" (Campisi 1977).

The powwow was a natural extension of the annual homecoming, affording a vehicle of expression for a new set of values within an established format. The group showed considerable skill both in publicizing the event and in mobilizing support within the Mashpee community. Wixon was able to get a series of articles, some under his byline, published in local papers, which, in addition to outlining the schedule of events, described the leaders, extolled their qualities of leadership and heritage, and, in general, placed a favorable imprimatur on the group and its activity.

The schedule of events for the 1928 powwow had an eclectic quality, a mixture that might seem incongruous. The powwow began on August 11 with a religious service at the Old Indian Church led by Supreme Sachem Leroy C. Perry. This was followed by speeches by A. Lawrence Lowell, president of Harvard University and a summer resident of Cotuit; W. H. Moorehead of the United States Board of Indian Commissioners; the local state representative; Stephen Peters, chairman of the Mashpee Board of Selectmen; and others. After the introductory speeches, the tribal reunion commenced, under the direction of Eben Queppish. This consisted of a peace pipe ceremony and speeches by the nation's leaders emphasizing their unity and identity as Wampanoags. The second day began with a commemoration of the death of King Philip in 1676 and ended with a ten-mile marathon and baseball games between the Mashpees and the Narragansetts and the married versus single women of the Mashpee tribe. On the thirteenth; the last day of the powwow, there was a beauty contest, won, naturally enough, by a Mashpee woman, and more games, singing, and dancing. Other aspects of Indian identity were incorporated, including ceremonies, the wearing of regalia, and a recounting of the long history of Mashpees and the Wampanoag presence in New England (New Bedford Sunday Standard, Aug. 11, 1929:30; Boston Evening Transcript, Aug. 14, 1929(3):1; Falmouth Enterprise, Aug. 15, 1929:1). This mixture of pan-Indian and local Mashpee features persisted in varying degrees and with shifting emphases for the next fifty years.

The fledgling organization was shocked by the death of Eben Queppish, who was killed in an automobile accident in January 1933, at the age of seventy-three. He was buried, in full regalia, in the Indian cemetery in Mashpee after a dual Christian-Indian ceremony attended by some two hundred mourners. Queppish was eulogized as "the greatest Indian leader in the Eastern states in the last fifty years" (New Bedford Standard Times, Jan. 11, 1933:3) and interred with what one observer called "a full Indian ceremony." Four pallbearers, dressed in regalia, carried the coffin the two hundred feet from the church to the grave, followed in double file by the mourners. There was a brief ceremony, and after committal each person passed by the grave and tossed a sprig of pine on the coffin.

A month after Queppish's death, some leaders of the Mashpee Wampanoags announced that they would perform dances and ceremonies that they said were both ancient and secret to prove "that the once mighty Wampanoags still live, still follow the customs, the traditions and adhere to the laws and legends of their ancestors" (ibid. Feb. 5, 1933:3). The group gave credit for the revival to Queppish, who was presented as having been the repository of the ancient Wampanoag beliefs and who, it was asserted, trained his nephew Clarence Wixon to be his successor as tribal spokesman. The ceremonies included what Wixon identified as an eagle dance, a discovery dance, and a victory dance, all reportedly handed down in secrecy for two hundred years. In its publicity, the group made a clear effort to present these activities as ancient and the revitalization as a renewal of interest among the predominantly younger members of the tribe.

The renewal, though political in nature, was not a challenge to the established tribal government of the Mashpees, but rather an effort to provide a parallel structure for perpetuating an Indian identity. The group was challenging the leadership of Perry for control of the Wampanoag Nation by establishing an alternative slate of officers.

> According to Chiefs Red Shell (Clarence Wixon) and High Eagle (William James), there are supposed to be from 12 to 23 officials of the tribe. The highest possible office is "medicine chief" which was held by the late Eben Queppish—the only Wampanoag to have the honor in the last 100 years. It is expected that it may be many years before the tribe has another. Next in rank the chief sachem and the chief sagamore, leaders of the entire tribe. Of equal rank with them is the chief medicine man. Under these

leaders are two overseers, one on the Cape and the other on Martha's Vineyard. They are not tribal chiefs but during their tenure of office have the title of "chief." Two medicine men serve each group under the direction of the chief medicine man, and each group has a treasurer who is a member of the tribe's finance committee. (Ibid.)

The February meeting signaled a split in the leadership of the nation into a "traditionalist" segment led by Haynes and a group led by Perry and Hammond. In death, Queppish became the vehicle by which Haynes and his supporters claimed control, and to sustain that claim, they claimed for Queppish special ties to the past. At issue, according to Haynes, was the practice of making public, at powwows, rites the group asserted were sacred, as well as the practice of allowing women to participate in councils (ibid.).

Haynes's claim to the title of chief was based, according to him, on his having won a ten-mile race in 1933 (*Boston Herald*, Apr. 11, 1935:11). He moved to consolidate his position at the August powwow by installing Oakes Coombs, an eighty-year-old Mashpee, as medicine man (*New Bedford Standard Times*, Aug. 19, 1933:1). But Perry refused to accept this installation, and in 1933 he removed Wixon as second in command and secretary of the Wampanoags. The following year Wixon resigned as Mashpee chief and historian, accusing Perry of actions in opposition to the purposes for which they had organized the nation, namely, the preservation of Wampanoag culture (*New Bedford Sunday Standard*, Aug. 5, 1934:23). The following year Perry ousted Haynes and reinstated Hammond as chief of the Mashpees, an action Haynes bitterly protested, demanding a vote of the full membership of the tribe (*Boston Herald*, Apr. 11, 1935:11). No meeting was held, Haynes continued to serve as chief, and in that capacity he made the Democratic governor of Massachusetts, James Curley, a tribal member. That was too much for the Wampanoag leaders, who had strong affinities for the Republican party. They held a meeting at the Mashpee town hall and announced, "We, the members and officers of the Mashpee Wampanoag tribe herein assembled, do hereby resolve that the public by these presents be shown that the so-called Chief Wild Horse is no official of the Wampanoag tribe of Mashpee. Our chiefs, duly elected, are Chief Ousa Mequin, Rev. Leroy C. Perry of Gay Head, Chief High Eagle, medicine man, William James, and Chief Drifting Goose, assistant medicine man, Ellsworth R. Oakley" (*Boston Globe*, May 14, 1936:2).

The statement did not indicate who held the Mashpee chieftainship, but it appears that Oakley carried out the responsibilities well into the 1940s. Haynes continued to assert his claim as Mashpee leader, but Perry's actions decisively ended the controversy.

Over the course of the ten years of bickering and dispute, the Wampanoag movement developed a structure that complemented the tribe-town government. But tribal government did not depend on this cultural revival, although the movement had a significant effect on the Mashpees' identity. For example, it drew them into contact with values and behaviors attributed to other Native Americans, many of which they borrowed and incorporated into their system of beliefs. In this, the Wampanoag movement was assisted by a generally favorable press, which gave them a forum for expression and a means to contact other interested parties. The system of leadership evolved rapidly through its principal means of expression and experimentation — the powwow. Although after 1927 the Mashpee leaders of the Wampanoag Nation took over many of the public aspects of the annual homecoming, the event remained a largely Mashpee occasion.

The emphasis on the modes of dress and dance of the Plains Indians, the eclectic nature of the political structure, and the cultural syncretism exhibited, although most apparent, were not the sole or even the most significant basis for the revitalization. Throughout the nineteenth and twentieth centuries the Mashpees had continued to practice their own forms of folk medicine, the most prominent practitioner being Matthias Amos, who died in the early 1920s (*Falmouth Enterprise*, Sept. 27, 1928:7). There were, as well, as host of folktales involving ghosts, witches, and a culture hero, Maushop, who, as the legends describe, created the lakes and ponds of Mashpee, as well as the offshore islands (Simmons 1986). The Mashpees were rich, too, in material culture. They made a wide variety of baskets, decorated with designs applied with a potato stamp. These included serving baskets, pack baskets, eel pots, and weirs, to mention a few. They salted and smoked herring and prepared corn in special ways (Tantaquidgeon 1935). Mashpee men hunted and fished together, generally to the exclusion of outsiders, and this provided nearly limitless opportunities to share and expand the folklore about the community.

Paradoxically, the most enduring and cohesive unit of Mashpee identity was the Indian church. From the time of its organization in the mid-seventeenth century, the church had been a focal point for the Indian community. With guidance from the ministry, the Mashpees had avoided involvement in King Philip's War in 1675–76. Through the church the Mashpees gained the title to the land and preserved their control. It was generally the ministers, many of whom were members of the tribe, who were instrumental in protecting that land base and tribal independence during the eighteenth century. The opposition to Massachusetts law in the 1830s centered in the church and led to the eviction of the Congregationalist minister and his replacement by the Baptist preacher Blind Joe Amos. It led also to the establishment of the Indian District.

The church was the center of community activity. The original building was constructed in 1684 near Santuit Pond and was remodeled in 1717. It was moved to its present location, nearer to the center of the town, in 1854 (Old Indian Meeting House 1923:4). Around 1900 the church was closed because of declining use. The cultural revival sparked by Simons, Queppish, and others, however, led to the reconstruction of the building, which was rededicated with elaborate ceremony, in 1923 (*Cape Cod Magazine*, Oct. 1923:10–11). Finally, in 1934, the members of the church adopted a new constitution for the parish, setting themselves apart from both the denominational churches and the town (*Boston Globe*, Mar. 13, 1934:17).

In the seventy years after the imposition of the town form

of government, the Mashpees' internal political system had undergone significant changes. Three important vectors of community organization emerged: the tribal government, as represented by the town, which dealt with external matters and provided the necessary mechanisms for internal regulation through a network of family-based leadership; the Wampanoag movement, which provided a more visible Indian identity as well as the means for cultural revival; and the church and Old Indian Meeting House, which emphasized the Mashpees' long tenure and religious tradition.

During this period, much of the Indian-owned land had been sold, and there had been a steady shift of the population from the southern portions of the town to the area of Mashpee Pond. Mashpees continued to think of the town as their property, and although much of the land had been sold, its resources — fish, shellfish, game, berries, and wood — remained available to tribal members. It was a nearly inexhaustible and free source of protein. The Mashpees could not conceive of the loss of these resources any more than they could conceive of the loss of political control. Thus they took no steps to ensure either their economic or political independence.

World War II brought the first breach to their insularity. Despite the war and its attendant shortages of fuel and building materials, there was an increase in the number of summer cottages, particularly along the bay areas. In addition, the federal government expanded Otis Air Force Base on the western side of the town, taking land from Mashpee. The result was an increase in population and employment. Following the war, Mashpee found itself a prime target for development. The long-dormant New Seabury Corporation, which owned some 2,700 acres of the town along its shoreline, began to develop first individual residences and later planned villages and condominiums. Augmented by other projects, the town's population expanded dramatically, from 434 in 1940 to 867 in 1960 (U.S. Bureau of the Census 1940, 1960). More significantly, the 1960 figures showed a shift to a white majority, 535 whites as compared with 342 nonwhites. By 1970, the population had reached 1,288 (ibid. 1970). The growth was so sudden that Indian leaders had little opportunity to assess its impact until the mid- 1970s, when it became evident in the voting booths. As Hutchins describes the situation:

> The political implications of Mashpee's building boom were obscured by the fact that whites had owned summer houses in Mashpee for decades. It was not immediately apparent that this time many homebuilders would make Mashpee their principal residence. Nor was it automatically assumed that the new white voters would upset the political applecart. The initial reaction of Mashpee's political establishment to sky-rocketing land values and rapid development of shorefront property was enthusiastic. More wealth in town meant a larger tax base, and this had been considered beneficial in previous years. Throughout the 1960's and early 1970's, the annual reports of Mashpee's Indian-majority Boards of Selectmen spoke almost lyrically of the soaring number and value of building permits issued during the past twelve months, and expressed pride that so many new people were discovering that Mashpee was a pleasant place to live. (1979: 160–61)

The pleasantness wore off quickly after 1970. The Mashpees maintained control of town government until 1968. In that year a second white selectman, Kevin O'Connell, was elected to serve with Leo Sweeney (white) and Frank Hicks (Indian). In 1972, Randolph Peters was elected to replace Sweeney and the Indian majority was restored, but not for long. Two years later, a white majority was elected and the Indians permanently lost control of the town government. In and of itself, the election of a white majority was not significant; what mattered was that the elections represented a polarization of the community into white and Indian, with each side enunciating different interests and concerns. For the whites, these concerns included protection of their newly acquired property from trespass and unfettered freedom to develop the land as they wished and to direct the town's services for their benefit. For the Mashpees, it meant the protection of their access to resources they considered inalienable, the right to travel the town's "ancient ways," and, most important, unlimited access to the beaches and bays. Their sense of identity depended on these rights. The two were mutually exclusive and incompatible, and conflict was inevitable if the Mashpees were to maintain their tribal identity.

After its frenetic and sometimes discordant beginnings, the Wampanoag movement achieved some semblance of stability during the 1940s. Ellsworth Oakley, Sr. (Drifting Goose), served as Mashpee chief until 1948, when, because of the requirements of his job, which necessitated long absences from the community, he stepped down. Earl Mills took over the responsibilities, although Elmer Hendricks, Sr., is said to have actually held the position. The matter was cleared up in 1956, when a group of tribal members petitioned Perry, the supreme sachem, to "bring about an election of a chief in Mashpee. We have had no local chief for some time — so are this Petition signed by Mashpee Indians — for the appointing of Mr. Earl Mills. . . . We consider him a necessary requisite to the further growth and interest of our people — if — we can persuade him that we need him" (signed by 56 Mashpees).

Perry replied to their request on September 2, 1956, as follows:

> On this date after Religious Services at the Old Indian Church at Mashpee, Mass. Rev. CC Wilson Rev. and Supreme Sachem Ousa Mequin = Yellow Feather — Pocasett — Wampanoag = did confirm and declare,— elected to the office of Chief of the Mashpee Indian Tribe according to a Petition by the majority of Families of Mashpee, Mass. and in accordance with a Council Meeting held at the Town Hall the night before Sat. the 1st of Sept.
>
> I, the undersigned Supreme Sachem of the Wampanoag Councils of Mass. do hereby present you with credentials confirming all that was necessary after the Supreme Sachem ceremonially confirmed you at the Church Ser-

vices. You received the Name = "Flying Eagle" and, as such
—you are in charge of all Council Meetings held by the
Indians of Mashpee, Mass. and none is above you in any
office.

To all concerned = Respect and obedience to the Chiefs
will is hereby ordered and the Blessing of the Great Spirit
requested on his years of Service Noosukkuhhum = I write
this new kenauau = to you—as, a Ourematin ut sachemoo
= Brother and Chief = to = Ptooeu Wampsi kook = Flying Eagle Wampanoag Council of Mashpee, Mass. Rev. +
Supreme Chief Sachem—Ousa Mequin Yellow Feather Po-
casset W. (Mashpee Wampanoag Tribal Council Minutes)

As a final step of validation, the appointment was confirmed at the next powwow.

For the next ten years Mills directed his attention to two
main projects: the continuance of the cultural revitalization
begun the previous decade and the restoration of the Old Indian Church, which had fallen into disrepair. In the first instance, he, with the assistance of tribal members, organized
classes in basket making, beadwork, singing and dancing, and
language. These efforts were financed through donations and
by a variety of fund-raising activities and were directed at train-
ing the youth. Mills was a physical education teacher in the
Falmouth School District and therefore had broad contact with
the Mashpee children and their parents. Although the efforts
were modest, they had an important effect on the identity of
a peer group that reached adulthood in the 1970s, the period
of schism within the town.

The church restoration was a more ambitious project, involving the raising of thousands of dollars. Mills joined the
other tribal members and through a variety of activities — sup-
pers, sales, raffles, and the like — collected sufficient money to
refurbish the church.

The Wampanoag Nation, too, was undergoing changes
in leadership. William James served as supreme medicine man
until his death in the mid-1960s. He was succeeded by Louis

Webquish, who died in 1976, and was, in turn, succeeded by John Peters. Perry continued to serve as supreme sachem into the 1960s. Upon his death he was succeeded by Lorenzo Jeffers of Gay Head.

Jeffers died in 1974, and very quickly a power struggle developed with four candidates seeking the office. None of the four was able to develop a broad base of support among the tribes, and to further complicate matters, there was no established mechanism for handling the competing claims to leadership. To resolve the impasse, the directors of the Mashpee Wampanoag Tribal Council, Inc., a recently formed unit of the tribe, and the Gay Head Tribal Council held a series of meetings to decide upon procedure. Finally, after several meetings, they agreed.

> It was the concensus [sic] of the opinion that we should attempt to select the Supreme Sachem through the democratic process, rather than to continue in the tradition of the past, when the position was chiefly obtained through hereditary lines. Others concurred with such notes as the fact that we should be willing to have different guidelines than those that had been defined in the past. It was pointed out that the things that affected Massasoit (seventeenth century Wampanoag Sachem) and his people were different than those that we encountered today, and that the election of a Supreme Sachem be updated. All were in agreement, although no vote was taken. (Ibid. Nov. 17, 1974)

The two tribal councils made the necessary arrangements for the election, preparing ballots and lists of eligible voters, sending out absentee ballots, appointing tellers, and setting the time and place for the election. The election was held on two days, May 3 and May 10, 1975, and the results were announced by the two tribal councils. Ellsworth Oakley, Jr. (Drifting Goose), won by a single vote, and this resulted in inevitable challenges. After considering the objections, the council affirmed the results, and Oakley became the supreme sachem. In the summer of 1977 the supreme sachem designated John Peters

(Slow Turtle) to be the supreme medicine man, thus confirming his authority and returning to a more informal consensual mode of selection.

The supreme medicine man is considered to be the nation's religious leader. He offers prayers at public meetings, leads tribal ceremonies, performs rites at weddings and funerals, gives names, and offers counseling to adults and children who seek his aid. His office is a primary means for Wampanoag cultural transmission, and he provides a link to the past because what he knows he is believed to have learned from former medicine men and tribal elders. He holds the view that part of what he knows comes directly from the Creator; he believes he was chosen by the Supreme Being and sees himself as His instrument.

According to the supreme medicine man, John Peters, the earth is the center of existence. The principal requisite for humanity is to maintain a balance with the earth. For everything that is taken, an equal amount must be returned. It falls to mankind to maintain this equilibrium, and to do so people must recognize, accept, and participate in what Peters and others consider the essence of existence — the medicine circle. From their viewpoint, everything in creation is part of a circle, and birth and death are but two benchmarks of the cycle, for everything springs from the earth and returns to it.

The two themes of balance and reciprocity find expression at every ceremony and public meeting, whether it be the opening of a tribal council meeting, a unity conference, a religious ceremony at the Old Indian Church, or a powwow. Though the primary concern of the medicine man, they also receive considerable attention from other leaders. Below are examples:

> Remember that the circle is always there and we must unite that we see again that which we had before. Everything in nature is round — only man has square things. Continue to think of the Medicine Circle to help us to help others — be others. Everything has a spirit — a use — a purpose. (John Peters, Medicine Man, Mashpee Powwow, July, 1977)

All living things have a spirit—everything a part of the same structure—everything is part of the medicine circle without end. . . . We have problems since the white man landed on our shores—destroyed our beliefs and softened our people. [But] the circle is mending. [When] we sit in a circle everything is truth. In the circle we must look at each other. We unite in the circle so the spirit can move. We think about a particular person because we feel we can heal that person. When we talk, we talk about we, not I, and no one is elevated above another whether chief or medicine man. (John Peters, interview, August 14, 1977)

The circle of love, brotherhood, and unity is mending. The time has come for all to get together. It is our last chance. As long as Indian people have the pipe [Calumet], we will have hope. This is our roots, this is our land. Here is the land of the aboriginal. There is no way we can fail. (Ellsworth Oakley, Jr., Supreme Sachem, Old Indian Meeting House, July 3, 1977)

We joined together in this small circle with the chiefs of the Wampanoags and with chiefs of other tribes, inside the larger circle which you are [referring to the attending public], to discuss the problems of our peoples. We smoke the pipe that the Creator may know of our message. The circle is unity, it is strength. It sustains us spiritually and in good will. It is here on our Mother Earth, from whom we get all, and to whom we give all, and to whom we all return. This is our great cycle, and we feel the strength of it and we join our hands to be part of the spirit of everyone. We ask you who have come here today to see this festival to be patient because we have serious work to do for our people. (Earl Mills, Mashpee Powwow, 1977)

Not every Mashpee is a professed and devoted follower of a traditionalist way, but individuals of other denominations generally believe in the efficacy of these teachings. It is not uncommon to find, for example, a Baptist parishioner speaking of the land in much the same manner as the traditionalists or acknowledging the leadership role of the Wampanoag Nation. In this context, one highly respected Baptist woman described the medicine man as a person who "is not concerned with physical cures. He's more involved with spiritual matters. He is the spiritual leader of the tribe" (Campisi fieldnotes 1977).

The role of chief in Mashpee is consistent with the proper role of a traditional leader in other Indian groups, one who leads by consensus. He is expected to eschew any implications of command and to depend instead on moral suasion to accomplish his aims or, more precisely, the aims of the group as they are made known to him. As he and others see it, his duties are to communicate the views of the Mashpees to other tribes; to provide counseling and guidance to tribal members, particularly the young; to represent the Mashpees at the Wampanoag councils; to assist in the resolution of internal disputes; and occasionally to represent the tribe in its relations with the non-Indian community.

Earl Mills, the chief of the Mashpees for the past twenty-five years, sees his position as one of conciliator, responsible for the maintenance of tribal cohesion. He operates largely on the basis of consensus derived from regular and informal contacts with the members of the Indian community. As one Mashpee put it, "As long as people are willing to follow, he'll lead" (ibid.).

The positions of sachem and medicine man evolved over at least a fifty-year period, and in the course of that time have been accepted and incorporated into the Indian community's value system. The nonassertive nature of these positions is, in part, a reflection of the values in the community, in part a belief in how leaders behaved in the distant past, and in part a result of the personalities of the individuals who have held the positions, particularly Mills and Peters. And in large measure, the positions have been shaped by the concerns that interest the leaders and the remedies available.

In contrast, the establishment of the Mashpee Wampanoag Tribal Council, Inc., came as a direct response to the Mashpees' imminent loss of control over town affairs. Though the

Wampanoag Nation leaders could enunciate values and provide leadership for community projects, they were incapable of meeting the challenge from the loss of political control.

This impending loss was perceived by a number of tribal members, including Amelia Peters Bingham, the daughter of Stephen Peters, in the early 1970s. Bingham had returned to Mashpee in 1964 after her husband's retirement from military service. He was appointed the town's police chief, and she turned her energies toward local projects. She became active in the town's bicentennial program, developing exhibits detailing the town's Indian heritage and, as part of the project, writing a town-tribal history. These interests led her into more ambitious projects, foremost among them the development of the Mashpee Wampanoag Museum. With considerable zeal and skill, she and others raised the funds to restore the building and, through solicited loans and gifts, filled it with a variety of exhibits. Her activities gained her statewide prominence, and in 1974, Governor Michael Dukakis appointed her as one of seven commissioners of Indian affairs for the state of Massachusetts.

Bingham and others were concerned with what they perceived as a threat to the Mashpee tribe and their way of life, not only by the loss of political control but by a growing insensitivity on the part of the white majority to their interests. Although several factors contributed to the decision to launch the incorporated group, the most compelling was the closing of the shoreline areas by developers, particularly New Seabury Corporation. The growth of this corporation had caused sufficient alarm by 1971 that the town voted to change its zoning law to forbid cluster development. The corporation took the town to court, arguing that it had a binding commitment under the previous law passed in 1963, which gave it a virtual carte blanche to develop as it pleased. In 1974, the County Court concurred and ruled that the changes were not applicable to New Seabury. The pace of enclosure quickened.

From the Mashpee point of view, the loss of control of the land base combined with the loss of free and unlimited access to resources severely threatened tribal identity. Over the years, the Mashpees had moved from the southern portions of the town to a concentration along two roads in the northeastern section. The realization that the political power in the town had shifted with the development of the southern portion that they had left and lost forced the tribe to adopt a new strategy to maintain its identity and influence. The remedy chosen was to form a tribal corporation.

The Mashpee Wampanoag Tribal Council, Inc., was chartered by the state of Massachusetts in 1974. It set as its principal objectives "to raise the socio-economic and spiritual level of the Mashpee Wampanoags;" to "assist in the quest for Self-Determination" through the preservation of the history, culture, and land; and to improve education and employment opportunities for tribal members (Wampanoag Tribal Council, Inc. 1974). To accomplish these goals, the constitution provided for a board of directors consisting of the elected president, vice-president, secretary, treasurer, historian, and other members of the tribe. In addition, the chief and medicine man were made ex officio members of the board.

The board of directors sets policy for the corporation. It determines priorities, directs tribally related activities, and administers federal and state funds for a variety of projects. In addition, the tribal council manages a fifty-five-acre plot purchased from the town in 1976. For its daily operation, the tribe has hired an administrator who takes direction from and is answerable to the board. In addition, the board has responsibility for compiling and maintaining the tribal membership list.

The chief officer of the council is the president, who is responsible for conducting meetings, making sure that various reports are filed on time and with the appropriate body, negotiating with other government agencies, and, in general, representing the Mashpees in their relations with other entities. Because of the tribe's bifurcated structure, there is the potential for conflict between the president and the chief. This has been significantly reduced by a quid pro quo; the chief is responsible for internal concerns special to the maintenance of the tribe and unique to it by virtue of the tribe's ethnic and cultural attributes, while the president exerts leadership in the area of Indian-white relations.

Once the tribal council had been incorporated, its members elected Russell Peters as its first president. Peters, the brother of Amelia and John, had recently returned to Mashpee after a career in industry. Articulate and outspoken, he became the principal spokesman for the Mashpee point of view. He also became one of the principal targets for the opponents of the land suit.

Not only was he subjected to criticism from the non-Indians within the town, but there were elements in the tribe that strongly challenged his leadership. On one side were individuals who were willing to accommodate the new political reality, the loss of control of the town government, to avoid reprisals. They held that Peters's approach was too confrontational and too extreme. At the opposite end were the younger members of the tribe, who, influenced by the growing pan-Indian movement, did not trust American courts and laws. They felt that the Creator would find a way to preserve the Wampanoag land and culture. Instead of taking the middle ground between two extremes, Peters became identified as a radical, trapped between two opposing forms of conservatism.

With the advent of the tribal corporation, many of the issues that concerned tribal members — access to the beaches, the closing of land by developers to hunting and fishing, and the destruction of the ancient ways — became issues for the tribal council to remedy. Even though the Mashpees held many of the elective offices in 1974, real political power had passed to the new residents, who had their own ideas about priorities and issues. Planning was already under way to move the center of Mashpee from the north end of the town, where most of the tribal members lived, to the southwestern part, where New Seabury owned a shopping center and most of the commercial property. In 1976, Peters and the tribal council established an office with funds received from the federal government. It quickly became the focus of the opposition to the changes occurring in Mashpee.

During the summer of 1976, incidents occurred which intensified the growing tensions between the tribe and the new town government. At the same time, a group of Mashpee young people were camping out one evening near Mashpee Pond. Suddenly, they were arrested by a squad of town police and accused of drumming and singing on town property. Although the individuals were eventually acquitted, the incident sent a clear message that the Mashpees no longer could expect special or even sympathetic treatment from the town leaders.

In the same year, Amelia Bingham, director of the Wampanoag Indian Museum, was dismissed by the selectmen and the museum closed. The action was clearly tied to the impending tribal lawsuits and was viewed by the tribe members as an effort to intimidate them. After several months the museum reopened with a non-Indian director. She met with the tribal council in an effort to gain its support but was rebuffed. She was told that the museum was being held hostage by the selectmen and that the tribal council could not and would not countenance such behavior.

Faced with unremitting opposition from the town government and a sizable portion of the non-Mashpee community, the tribal council became a focal point of tribal identity. It defended tribal values and attitudes, particularly with regard to the land and resources, and it exerted pressure and influence over its constituents. For example, when the defendant's expert witness, Jeanne Guillemin, attempted to survey the attitudes of the Mashpees, the tribal council prevented the members from participating. Throughout the trial period the tribal council acted as the official voice of the group, and by 1976 it had supplanted the town as the agent of the tribe.

For most of the one hundred years covered in this chapter the Mashpees were in control of their affairs. The imposition of the town form of government and its acceptance by the Mashpees did not mean they had been assimilated into the general population any more than their acceptance of Christian belief two hundred years before had marked the death knell of their ethnic identity. It is a common phenomenon for Ameri-

can Indian communities to acquiesce in the imposition of political structures, for example, the stilted constitutions and alien
business committees forced on tribes by the Indian Reorganization Act as a requisite for federal recognition.

Within the framework of the government imposed by the
state, the Mashpees operated to serve the interests of tribal members. Zimmerman was correct in observing that the Mashpees
were manipulating the powers of town government to benefit
tribal members and that they were maintaining distinct social
boundaries drawn along kinship lines. Access to power and
the benefits derived from it were dependent on family ties, and
this remained unchanged throughout the tribe's history.

Until the early 1900s, the Mashpees' use of the term *Indian* had a narrow and specific meaning. It is ironic that the
individuals who left the community to find work and education should be instrumental in broadening the Mashpees' sense
of their Indian identity. Yet without this experience, they would
have been no less Indian. Their ethnicity depended on their
long tenure, their social insularity, their sense of family, their
economic stability, and, of course, their political independence.
In these conditions there was little need for overt displays of
Indianness. Most outsiders who knew them knew they were
Indians. Only when their identity was threatened in the 1970s
did the tribe's cohesion manifest itself. If the Mashpees possessed a failing in the years before 1970, it was that they so
adapted the imposed institutions to their own needs and devices that they appeared to the uninitiated to have been co-
opted themselves.

❖ 7 ❖

THE LEGACY OF THE TRIAL

MANY OF THE MASHPEES received Judge Skinner's dismissal with shocked disbelief, others with bitter resignation. Most of the tribal leaders had grown up in the Indian community and had lived there all their lives. They were older, respected citizens, church members, and civic leaders. They viewed the trial as a means to acknowledge the obvious — that they were Indians and members of a tribe that had occupied the area for 350 years and continued to occupy it, even though they had been victims of an illegal alienation. In that innocence bred of public school civic lessons, they felt sure they would triumph and that their claims would be vindicated by an impartial tribunal in a neutral court. They were bewildered by the rules that had directed them to demonstrate an identity no one had previously questioned. They were hurt by the repeated attacks on their credibility and outraged by the racial innuendos that had permeated the proceedings. They could not fathom the justice of a system that said, in effect, you may have a legitimate claim to the land, but you can't bring it because we don't believe you are who you say you are. When the jury found that the Mashpees were not a tribe, their exasperation and frustration were succinctly expressed by their attorney Lawrence Shubow, who, on hearing the court's ruling,

151

told a reporter: "We have a mystery. We have a tribe that was in existence in 1834. What became of it? Did it go into orbit? It's hard to kill a tribe, even legally" (*Boston Globe*, Jan. 7, 1978).

Other Mashpees, younger and less idealistic, had doubted from the beginning that the tribe could (or would) receive a fair hearing. In their view, the claim was too large and threatened an American article of faith, the inviolability of private property. They asked how the tribe could receive a fair hearing from an all-white jury in Boston, the city that had vehemently defied another federal judge's efforts to desegregate its schools. These young men and women were better acquainted than their parents with the problems facing Indians in other parts of the nation. They were part of an emerging transcultural, pan-Indian militant religious movement spreading across "Indian Country," bringing new perspectives to Indian history and new vitality to Indian beliefs and traditions.

By contrast, as one might expect, the majority of the non-Indian residents in Mashpee were ecstatic over the results. Selectmen George Benway and Kevin O'Connell saw the decision as a vindication of their economic vision. With the cloud over land titles removed, they and others could pursue the marketing of Mashpee. While he spoke of putting "the town together again," O'Connell was emphatic about the feelings within the town toward the Mashpees. "I won't lie to you, it's [animosity] there, the two most important things to a person are his family and his home. You threaten either one, and you're going to get a very angry person" (ibid. Jan. 8, 1978).

The Mashpees appealed Judge Skinner's decision, but on February 13, 1979, a three-member panel of the U.S. Court of Appeals upheld the lower court's decision. Writing for the panel, Judge Frank J. Coffin found "that the Mashpees have lost this case represents not a failure of the law to protect Indians in changing times, but rather a failure of the evidence to show that this group was an object of the protective laws" (U.S. Court of Appeals for the First Circuit 1979:21).

The selectmen were elated by the Court of Appeals ruling; the Mashpees were disappointed.

"Obviously, I'm happy," [Selectmen] Benway said. "It confirms our belief from the beginning that there was no merit to the claim of tribal existence, and there was no valid claim of tribal existence, and there was no valid claim to the land in Mashpee."

"In August 1976 it was the plaintiff who chose to go to court and have the merits decided. I can remember as defendants that we had confidence then in the court system. We knew all the facts would be introduced and objectively assessed." (*Falmouth Enterprise*, February 16, 1979)

The Mashpees appealed once more, this time to the U.S. Supreme Court, which denied certiorari in October 1979. It appeared that the tribe had reached the end of the judicial line.

While the appeal process was going on, the tribe, with the assistance of NARF, commenced preparation of a petition for federal acknowledgment. In 1978, almost coincidentally with the verdict in the case, the Department of the Interior published regulations prescribing seven criteria necessary to demonstrate that an Indian group had a federal relationship. By the summer of 1980, the NARF researcher had completed a first draft of a petition and was working on the study of the contemporary community and political system of the tribe. When the selectmen became aware of the tribe's intention to apply for federal acknowledgment, they issued the following statement: "We intend to oppose rigorously this application and thereby hopefully preclude any new litigation with the Mashpee Indians" (*Cape Cod Times*, July 2, 1981).

Before NARF could complete the petition, however, the tribe changed direction. Upon the advice of Robert C. Hahn, a local attorney, tribal members from a number of groups, including Mashpees, instituted another suit for land in the towns of Mashpee, Bourne, Plymouth, and Fall River and Gay Head, Tisbury, and Chappaquidick on Martha's Vineyard. The claim encompassed some twenty-four thousand acres. This action was strongly opposed by the NARF attorney assigned to the case, Arlinda F. Locklear. She argued that the issues raised by Hahn were no different from the ones raised in the first case and that the tribe would ultimately fail. Unable to convince the tribe that its best interests lay in completing the petition and achieving federal acknowledgment, NARF withdrew from the case (more precisely, it was fired).

While not a plaintiff in the case, the Mashpee Wampanoag Tribal Council, Inc., supported it, although its board of directors was on record as being in opposition. "'The tribal council voted to go along with it,'" Ms. [Hannah] Averett [tribal president] said. "'The rest of the board felt if those people voted for it, then we had to go along. There was nothing that one or two of us could do about it'" (ibid. Dec. 29, 1981).

Hahn based his suit on the contention that the lands in question were Indian lands in 1790 and thus were protected by the Indian Trade and Intercourse Act. He argued that the suit was brought by individuals as well as the tribes. Further, he asserted that the Mashpees were a tribe by law because there is no act of Congress terminating a federal relationship with them. Therefore, he concluded, a trial of the facts was unnecessary (Hahn, 1986). Hahn also asked Judge Skinner to recuse himself, arguing that he "has not shown himself to be an impartial judge in this suit because of his involvement in the 1976 Mashpee Indian suit" (*Cape Cod Times*, Sept. 11, 1982).

Judge Skinner refused to remove himself from the case and in June 1983 dismissed the complaint. Hahn promptly appealed to the U.S. Court of Appeals, which heard arguments in March 1983 and upheld the dismissal as well as Skinner's refusal to recuse himself. Nonetheless, the case dragged on through the courts for another three years. Finally, in 1986, Judge Skinner dismissed the remaining issues of the case, those dealing with the lands outside of Mashpee. In the meantime, the Mashpee Wampanoag Tribal Council, Inc., had rehired NARF to complete its petition for federal acknowledgment.

Despite the dismissals, the struggles between the town of Mashpee and the Mashpee tribe continued. At every point of contact and at every opportunity, the town's leaders insisted that no tribe existed and that the Mashpees were not Indians. In 1977, the Mashpee Board of Assessors reassessed the fifty-five acres that had been sold by the town to the tribe in 1975 for $500. The reassessed value was set at $158,480 and a tax of $2,266.26 was levied. NARF attorney Barry Margolin argued that the amount of the assessment was unreasonable given the severe restrictions in the deed, that the tribe was protected by federal law, that the tribe was a nonprofit entity incorporated under state law, and that the tax was in retaliation for the land suit. The State Appellate Tax Board ruled in favor of the tribe (*Cape Cod Times*, May 3, 1979), but the matter was appealed to the state's highest court, which reversed part of the finding and sent the matter back to the Appellate Tax Board (*Cape Cod Times*, Jan. 11, 1980). Finally, the matter was settled when the board ruled in favor of the tribe on the basis of its status as a tax-exempt corporation. The bitterness and hostility remained.

In the process of redefining the town of Mashpee, the selectmen shifted its government offices southward, closer to the geographic and demographic center. The elementary school in the Indian portion of the town was converted to town offices, and a new one was built in the southwestern part of the town. The post office was moved to the traffic circle, again in the southern part. The firehouse in Mashpee village, across the street from the former elementary school, was closed and a new one constructed further to the south.

These movements left two buildings empty, the firehouse and the town hall. The tribal council, needing more space and desirous of preserving the old town hall, applied to the board of selectmen, offering a ten-year lease and committing the tribe to raise the funds for its renovation. The selectmen expressed concern that a lease to the tribe might have some undesirable effect on the tribe's claims to federal recognition and thus its land claim. Selectmen Benway told the tribe, "We want to know what it (this proposed lease) would mean in terms of the old (Indian land claims suit) and any new suits and federal recognition" (*Cape Cod Times*, Jan. 8, 1981). In the end, the firehouse and the town hall were razed, eliminating two of the most important Indian institutions.

There were other disputes and instances which tribal mem-

bers interpreted as arrogations. For example, the tribal members took extreme umbrage to town officials treating the Indian cemetery as town property and ignoring the Mashpees'
special interests in the property. The tribe's anger and frustration were expressed by its president, Joan Tavares, in a letter
to the editor:

> No room in the cemetery? No room from whom? I'm
> wondering where that cemetery is located? I know of no
> other of size in Mashpee than the old Indian Cemetery
> [sic] also known as the Old Indian Burial Grounds.
>
> It is no secret that some elected officials and some peo-
> ple in this town would find it very convenient to forget
> that Mashpee is or ever was an Indian town. (Witness the
> efforts to tear down or name any building of historical
> value from the old Mashpee center of town.) Now, how
> easily the "Indian" has been taken out of the cemetery title.
>
> Nowhere in the eleven times that the word cemetery
> has been mentioned in your article has the word "Indian"
> been attached. This is even more preposterous — consider-
> ing for years that the old Indian cemetery has been pointed
> out by Capesters and travelers as a direction landmark
> almost as commonly as one says "North and South."
> Think Mashpee and you think "old Indian cemetery."
>
> Sadly, it is now "our cemetery" to elected officials and
> sadly, the concern is for other people getting into the ceme-
> tery. Nary a thought to the Mashpee Wampanoags whose
> ancestors (and friends) have rested here since the sixteen
> hundreds and for whom the cemetery was designed. What
> of our plans to rest beside our loved ones? We maintain
> and firmly believe the old Indian cemetery was, is, and
> always will be our burial grounds.
>
> A few short months ago we protested the erection of
> a town maintenance building on our cemetery land and
> produced deeded rights which were ignored. Aside from
> ignoring us when we claimed this area as cemetery land,
> where was the foresightedness of elected officials in pro-
> jecting the need to keep this as cemetery land?
>
> So greedy have town planners been to press forward

with condos and golf course, that never a thought was given that a natural process to life is dying, and that these newcomers would need a last resting place. Just as never a thought was given to all other pressing needs such as water, sewage, and disposal. We are beginning to reap the folly of that greed. (*Mashpee Messenger*, Mar. 19, 1986)

Another controversy was brewing, one involving a fundamental issue to native people and an article of faith to non-Indians: the right to fish and hunt without restriction. In the summer of 1984, four members of the tribe were arrested for taking shellfish without a permit and for exceeding the limits set by the state. The four were tried in a county court and were defended by Lew Gerwitz, an attorney who specializes in Indian rights cases. Gerwitz argued that the court had no jurisdiction and that tribal members had a right to take shellfish "that precedes the Union." During the trial, he called a number of witnesses who attested that tribal members had exercised their rights to hunt and fish continuously since the earliest contact with Europeans and that fishing (and, by implication, hunting) were essential aspects of tribal culture and heritage, providing income for some and a ready food source for the rest. The assistant district attorney's response was to tell the court, "They are not a tribe, they are individuals who are assimilated into American society and culture" (*Cape Cod Times*, Sept. 15, 1984).

Judge Brian Rowe took the case under advisement and on October 2 dismissed all the charges against the four defendants. Tribal members saw the judge's decision as a vindication; the assistant district attorney viewed it differently: "Only these particular defendants in this particular instance were let off the hook. It does not bind any other judge. It has no precedential value" (ibid. Oct. 3, 1984).

The following year the tribal council supported a compromise aimed at resolving the stalemate between it and the town. Under the compromise the town would recognize an aboriginal right to shellfish, and the tribe would agree that its members would show the shellfish warden a tribal membership card in lieu of a license. The proposed compromise was submitted to the selectmen by the shellfish commission, but it was promptly tabled until the selectmen could receive a legal opinion from their attorneys. Benway expressed the town's concerns, which verged on paranoia, saying that he did not favor special treatment for any group. He added, "I do not know when we get into cases of aboriginal rights" (*Falmouth Enterprise*, Sept. 20, 1985).

In the course of their struggle to maintain their identity, secure acknowledgment of their status as a federally recognized tribe, and recover their land base, the Mashpees have experienced nearly every phase of Indian history. Their history has been, in microcosm, the history of American Indians generally. Almost from first contact they were "blessed" with missionaries and land speculators. They maintained their language well into the eighteenth century (Goddard and Bragdon 1988) and aspects of their aboriginal cultural values and beliefs to the present (Simmons 1986). Their political structure changed at the whim of the colony and state, but the political system remained surprisingly constant because the fabric of the community remained constant. The shift to Christian doctrines, the imposition of plantation, district, and town forms of government, the adoption of English as the principal language, the occasional adoption of outsiders to the membership of the community, and even the loss of title to the land and the loss of political control of the town government did not alter the essential character of the Mashpee tribe. These were and are cultural veneers; the tribal core remains the closeness of family ties, the sense of a common history and heritage, the attachment to ancestral land, even though it is no longer theirs to control, the closed nature of tribal membership, the intimacy of social relations, the differential treatment accorded members and nonmembers, and, above all, the sense of themselves as a unique social and political entity. It is ironic that the efforts of the town's leaders and lawyers over the past ten years to deny the existence of the tribe have only reinforced their sense of solidarity.

Works Cited

Index

WORKS CITED

Apes, William
1979   *Indian Nullification of the Unconstitutional Laws of Massachusetts Relative to the Mashpee Tribe; or, The Pretended Riot Explained.* 1835. Reprint. Stanfordville, N.Y.: Earle M. Coleman.

ARM = Acts and Resolves of Massachusetts
1788   An Act for the Better Regulation of the Indian, Mulattoe and Negro Proprietors in Marshpee, in the County of Barnstable. Chapter 2.

1792   [Petition of Walter Spooner and Joseph Nye, Guardians, to the Senate and House of the Commonwealth of Massachusetts]. Chapter 148.

1795   [Address of Gideon Hawley] To the Honorable Senate and the Honorable House of Representatives in the Commonwealth of Massachusetts. Chapter 20.

1796   An Act Specially Providing for the Removal of Poor Persons from the District of Marshpee, who have no Legal settlement there. Chapter 23.

1807   [Petition of Mashpees] To the Honourable the Senate and House of Representatives of the Commonwealth of Massachusetts, in General Court Assembled. Chapter 109.

1808   An Act in addition to, and repealing part of the first section of an act, entitled, "An act for the better regulating of the Indian, Mulatto, and Negro proprietors and inhabitants of the plantation, called Marshpee, in the county of Barnstable, and for other purposes." Chapter 108.

1818   Resolve on the petition of William Mingo and others, Indians, on Marshpee Plantation. Chapter 89.

1819   An Act in addition to the several acts respecting the Indians and other persons, Proprietors and Residents on the Plantations of Mashpee and Herring Pond, so called. Chapter 105.

1834   An Act to Establish the District of Marshpee. Chapter 166.

1835   Address by Governor Davis to the Massachusetts Legislature Delivered January 13, 1835.

1840   An Act Concerning the District of Mashpee. Chapter 65:210–11.

1842   An Act Conerning the District of Mashpee. Chapter 72: 522–27.

1853   An Act to Abolish the Office of Commissioner of Mashpee. Chapter 186:466–68.

1862   An Act Concerning the Indians of the Commonwealth. Chapter 184:149–51.

1863   An Act in Relation to the District of Mashpee. Chapter 183:494–95.

1864   An Act to Protect the Trout Fishing in Mashpee. Chapter 150:91–92.

1867   An Act to Incorporate the Marshpee Manufacturing Company. Chapter 41:491–92.

1869   An Act to Enfranchise the Indians of the Commonwealth. Chapter 463:780–82.

1870   An Act to Incorporate the Town of Mashpee. Chapter 293:213–15.

ARMB = Acts and Resolves of the Province of Massachusetts Bay 1692–1702 *Acts, Laws and Resolves of Massachusetts Bay Colony.*

Barnstable Patriot
Jan. 5, 1886

Barnstable Patriot Supplement
May 2, 1921

Barth, Fredrik
1969   *Ethnic Groups and Boundaries.* Boston: Little, Brown.

Boston Evening Transcript
1929–39

Boston Globe
1923–88

Boston Herald
1932–36

Boston Morning Globe
Nov. 13, 1931

Boston Post
Mar. 17, 1932

Boston Traveler
1930–36

Bradford, William
1908   *History of Plymouth Plantation, 1606–1646.* Edited by
            William T. Davis. New York: Charles Scribner's Sons.

Brasser, Ted J. C.
1971   "The Coastal Algonkians: People of the First Frontiers."
            In *North American Indians in Historical Perspective,*
            edited by Eleanor B. Leacock and Nancy O. Lurie, pp.
            64–91. New York: Random House.

Brodeur, Paul
1978   "A Reporter at Large (Mashpee, Massachusetts)." *New
            Yorker,* Nov. 6, 1978, pp. 62–150.

1985   *Restitution: The Land Claims of the Mashpee, Passa-
            maquoddy, and Penobscot Indians of New England.*
            Boston: Northeastern University Press.

Campisi, Jack
1977–89   Ethnographic fieldnotes. Manuscript in Campisi's
            possession.

1979   "Foreword." In *Indian Nullification of the Unconstitu-
            tional Laws of Massachusetts Relative to the Mashpee
            Tribe: or, The Pretended Riot Explained.* 1835. Edited
            by William Apes, pp. v–x. Stanfordville, N.Y.: Earle M.
            Coleman.

Cape Cod Magazine
1923–26

Cape Cod Times
Oct. 21, 1977

Champlain, Samuel de
1922–36   *The Works of Samuel de Champlain.* 1626. Edited by
            Henry P. Biggar. 6 vols. Toronto: Champlain Society.

Cohen, Felix
1942   *Handbook of Federal Indian Law.* Facsimile ed. Albu-
        querque: Univ. of New Mexico Press.

Clifford, James
1988   *The Predicament of Culture: Twentieth-Century Eth-
        nography, Literature, and Art.* Cambridge, Mass.: Har-
        vard Univ. Press.

Dermer, Thomas
1906   "To His Worshipfull Friend M. Samuel Purchas,
        Preacher of the Word, at the Church a Little Within
        Ludgate, London." In Samuel Purchas, *Hakluytus Post-
        humus or Purchas His Pilgrimes*, 19:129–34. Glasgow:
        James MacLehose and Sons.

Falmouth Enterprise
1928–87

Freeman, James
1815   "A Description of Mashpee, in the County of Barn-
        stable, September 16th, 1802." *Massachusetts Historical
        Society Collections*, 2d ser., 3:1–12.

Fried, Morton
1975   "The Myth of Tribe." *Natural History* 84(4):12–20.

Goddard, Ives
1978   "Eastern Algonquian Languages." In *Handbook of
        North American Indians*, Vol. 15, *Northeast*, William C.
        Sturtevant, gen. ed., Bruce G. Trigger, vol. ed., pp. 70–
        77. Washington, D.C.: Smithsonian Institution.

Goddard, Ives, and Kathleen J. Bragdon
1988   *Native Writings in Massachusetts.* 2 vols. Philadelphia:
        American Philosophical Society.

Gookin, Daniel
1970   *Historical Collections of the Indians in New England.*
        1792. Edited by Jeffrey H. Fiske. N.p.: Towtaid.

Gunter, William R.
July 15, 1977   Press Conference. Transcript for the Office of the White House Press Secretary.

Hahn, Robert
1986   Reply Brief for Plaintiff, Appellate. U.S. Court of Appeals. First Circuit 86-1615.

Hallett, Benjamin
1834   *Argument of Benjamin Hallett, Counsel for the Memorialists of the Marshpee Tribe, Before a Joint Committee of the Legislature of Massachusetts.* Boston: J. Howe.

Harvard College Papers
1838   Letter from the District Selectmen to the President and Fellows of Harvard College, Jan. 1. Vol. 17, Document UAI 5.125, Harvard University Archives, Cambridge, Mass.

Harvard University
1836   Minutes of May 19, 1836. Vol. 7, Document UAI 5.302, Corporation Records, pp. 425, 429–35, Harvard University Archives, Cambridge, Mass.

Hutchins, Francis G.
1979   *Mashpee: The Story of Cape Cod's Indian Town.* West Franklin, N.H.: Amarta Press.

Jameson, J. Franklin, ed.
1959   *Narratives of New England, 1609–1664.* 1909. Reprint. New York: Barnes and Noble.

Jennings, Francis
1975   *The Invasion of America: Indians, Colonialism, and the Cant of Conquest.* Chapel Hill: Univ. of North Carolina Press.

Kearful, Jerome
1939   "Mashpee Sticks to Old Time Practices." *Boston Evening Transcript,* Aug. 17.

Kroeber, Alfred
1955   "Nature of the Landholding Group." *Ethnohistory* 2: 303–14.

Mashpee Messenger
1986   "It's 'Indian Cemetery'." Mar. 19.

Mashpee Tribal Minutes
1953–74   Mashpee Wampanoag Tribal Office, Mashpee, Mass.

Mashpee Wampanoag Tribal Council Minutes
1974–80   Mashpee Wampanoag Tribal Office, Mashpee, Mass.

MA = Massachusetts Archives, Boston, Mass.
Dec. 29,   [Petition of the Indian Proprietors of Mashpee, So
1753   Called]. 32:424–26a.
            Acts of 1788. May Sess. Chapter 2.

1760   [Petition of Reuben Cognehew]. 33:146–48.

MHS = Massachusetts Historical Society, Boston
1760–1807 Gideon Hawley Manuscripts.

1790   S. P. Savage Manuscripts.

1792–1915 Collections. 10 series. 70 vols. Cambridge and Boston:
            The Society.

Massachusetts House of Representatives
1827   "Committee Report to the Massachusetts House of Rep-
            resentatives." 68:1–12.

1839   [The Joint Special Committee Report on the petition of
            Ebenezer Attaquin, and forty others, of the Marshpee
            Indians, and the remonstrance of the Reverend Phineas
            Fish.] No. 72.

1849   "Report of the Commissioners Relating to the Condi-
            tion of the Indians of Massachusetts." 46:1–67.

1855   [No title]. 192:1–9.

1869a   "Hearing Before the Committee on Indians." 502:3–34.

1869b   [No title]. 483:1–26.

1878   [No title]. 238:2–11.

1879   "Report of a Committee of the Massachusetts Legisla-
            ture." 72:2–31.

Massachusetts Senate
1834   "Document Relative to the Mashpee Indians." 14:1–43.

1835   "Document Relating to Marshpee District." 8:1–11.

1835   Governor's Address to the Massachusetts Legislature.
            Jan. 13.

1853   "Commissioner's Report (1852)." 11:1–13.

1861   "Report to the Governor and Council, Concerning the
            Indians of the Commonwealth, Under the Act of April 6,
            1959," by John Milton Earle. Boston: William White,
            Printer to the State.

1878   [No title]. No. 238.

Mills, Earl
1977   Address. Mashpee Powwow. Mashpee, Mass. July 3.
Morse, Jedidiah
1822   *A Report to the Secretary of War of the United States,
            on Indian Affairs, Comprising a Narrative of a Tour
            Performed in the Summer of 1820, Under a Commis-
            sion of the President of the United States, for the Pur-
            pose of Ascertaining, for the Use of the Government,
            the Actual State of the Indian Tribes in Our Country.*
            New Haven: S. Converse.
New Bedford Evening Standard
Mar. 17, 1932
New Bedford Standard Times
Jan. 11; Feb. 5; and Aug. 19, 1933
New Bedford Sunday Standard
1923–34
Nichols, Roger L.
1988   "Something Old, Something New: Indians Since World
            War II." In *The American Indian Experience*, edited by
            Philip Weeks, pp. 292–310. Arlington Heights, Ill.:
            Forum Press.
Oakley, Ellsworth, Jr.
1977   Address. Old Meeting House, Mashpee, Mass. July 3.
Old Indian Meeting House at Mashpee
1923   Library of Cape Cod History and Genealogy. Yar-
            mouth, Mass.: C. W. Swift, Publisher and Printer.
PCR = Nathaniel B. Shurtleff and David Pulsifer, eds.
1855–61   *Records of the Colony of New Plymouth in New
            England.* 12 vols. in 10. Boston: W. White.
Peters, John
1977   Interview with Jack Campisi. Mashpee, Mass. Aug. 4.
Purchas, Samuel
1905–7   *Hakluytus Posthumus or Purchas, His Pilgrimes.* 1625.
            4 vols. Reprint. Glasgow: J. MacLehose and Sons.
Rothery, Rosamond Pentecost
1903   "A Forgotten Corner of Cape Cod." *Bourne Independent.*
Sahlins, Marshall
1961   "The Segmentary Lineage: An Organization of Preda-
            tory Expansion." *American Anthropologist* 63:322–43.

1968　　　*Tribesmen.* Englewood Cliffs, N.J.: Prentice-Hall.

Sahlins, Marshall, and Elman Service
1960　　　*Evolution and Culture.* Ann Arbor: University of Michigan Press.

Salwen, Bert
1978　　　"Indians of Southern New England and Long Island: Early Period." In *Handbook of North American Indians,* Vol. 15, *Northeast,* William C. Sturtevant, gen. ed., Bruce G. Trigger, vol. ed., pp. 160–76. Washington, D.C.: Smithsonian Institution.

Service, Elman
1958　　　*Profiles in Ethnology.* New York: Harper & Row.

1962　　　*Primitive Social Organization.* New York: Random House.

1966　　　*The Hunters.* Englewood Cliffs, N.J.: Prentice-Hall.

1971　　　*Primitive Social Organization: An Evolutionary Perspective.* 2d ed. New York: Random House.

Simmons, William S.
1986　　　*Spirit of the New England Tribes: Indian History and Folklore, 1620–1984.* Hanover, N.H.: Univ. Press of New England.

Snow, Dean
1978　　　"Late Prehistory of the East Coast." In *Handbook of North American Indians,* Vol. 15, *Northeast,* William C. Sturtevant, gen. ed., Bruce G. Trigger, vol. ed., pp. 58–69. Washington, D.C.: Smithsonian Institution.

1980　　　*Archaeology of New England.* New York: Academic Press.

Soper, Grace Weld
1890　　　"Among the Friendly Indians at Mashpee." *New England Magazine, An Illustrated Monthly* n.s., 2:277–79.

Speck, Frank
1928a　　"Territorial Subdivisions and Boundaries of the Wampanoag, Massachusett, and Nauset Indians." *Museum of the American Indian, Heye Foundation, Indian Notes and Monographs, Misc. ser. 44.* New York.

1928b　　"Native Tribes and Dialects of Connecticut: A Mohegan-Pequot Diary." In *43d Annual Report of the Bureau of*

American Ethnology for the Years 1925–1926, pp. 199–287. Washington, D.C.: Government Printing Office.

Stiles, Ezra
1916   *Extracts from Itineraries and Other Miscellanies of Ezra Stiles, D.C., LL.D., 1755–1794, with a Selection from His Correspondence.* Edited by Franklin B. Dexter. New Haven: Yale Univ. Press.

Sturtevant, William C.
1983   "Tribes and State in the Sixteenth and Twentieth Centuries." In *The Development of Political Organization in Native North America, 1979 Proceedings of the American Ethnological Society,* edited by Elisabeth Tooker, pp. 3–16. Washington, D.C.: The American Ethnological Society.

Swanton, John R.
1952   "Indian Tribes of North America." *Bureau of American Ethnology Bulletin 145.* Washington, D.C.: Government Printing Office.

Tantaquidgeon, Gladys
1935   Mashpee. Record Group 75. File G74-1935-150. National Archives, Washington, D.C.

TR = Town Reports
1870–1979 Annual Reports of the Town Officers of the Town of Mashpee.

TT = Trial Transcript
1977–78   *Mashpee Tribe* v. *Town of Mashpee.* 43 vols.

U.S. Bureau of the Census
    1940–1970 Census of Population, by County. Bureau of the Census, Department of Commerce.

U.S. House of Representatives Resolution 108.

Wampanoag Tribal Council, Inc.
1974   Constitution and By-Laws of the Mashpee Wampanoag Tribal Council, Inc. Manuscript Mashpee Wampanoag Tribal Office, Mashpee, Mass.

Winslow, Edward
1910   "Winslow's Relation." 1624. In *Chronicles of the Pilgrim Fathers,* edited by John Masefield, pp. 267–357. London: J. M. Dent; New York: E. P. Hutton.

Wroth, Lawrence C.
1970   *The Voyages of Giovanni de Verrazzano, 1524–1528.*
          New Haven: Yale Univ. Press.
Zimmerman, Carle C.
1938   *The Changing Community.* New York: Harper and
          Brothers.
Mar. 26, 1979 Interview. Gilmanton, N.H.

INDEX

THE MASHPEE INDIANS
was composed in 11 on 13 Palatino on Digital Compugraphic equipment
by Metricomp;
with display type in Neuland Inline by Dix Type;
printed by sheet-fed offset on 55-pound Glatfelter Antique Cream
and Smyth-sewn and bound over binder's boards in Joanna Arrestox B
by Maple-Vail Book Manufacturing Group, Inc.;
with dust jackets printed in 2 colors by Johnson City Publishing;
and published by
SYRACUSE UNIVERSITY PRESS
SYRACUSE, NEW YORK 13244-5160

THE Iroquois AND THEIR NEIGHBORS

LAURENCE M. HAUPTMAN, *Series Editor*

This series presents a wide range of scholarship—archaeology, anthropology, history, public policy, sociology, women's studies—that focuses on the indigenous peoples of Northeastern North America. The series encourages more awareness and a broader understanding of the Iroquois Indians—the Mohawk, Oneida, Onondaga, Cayuga, Seneca, and Tuscarora—and their Native American neighbors and provides a forum for scholars to elucidate the important contributions of the first Americans from prehistory to the present day.

Selected titles in the series include:

12/13/91